T0305557

Making Sense of Culture

**Cross-Cultural Expeditions
and Management Practices
of Self-Initiated Expatriates
in the Foreign Workplace**

Making Sense of Culture

Cross-Cultural Expeditions and Management Practices of Self-Initiated Expatriates in the Foreign Workplace

Norhayati Zakaria

Routledge
Taylor & Francis Group

LONDON AND NEW YORK

First published 2019 by Routledge

2 Park Square, Milton Park, Abingdon, Oxon OX14 4RN

605 Third Avenue, New York, NY 10017

Routledge is an imprint of the Taylor & Francis Group, an informa business

First issued in paperback 2021

Publisher's Note

The publisher has gone to great lengths to ensure the quality of this reprint but points out that some imperfections in the original copies may be apparent.

ISBN-13: 978-1-138-49076-5 (hbk)
ISBN-13: 978-1-03-217796-0 (pbk)
DOI: 10.4324/9781351034586

Library of Congress Cataloging-in-Publication Data

Names: Norhayati Zakaria, 1969- author.
Title: Making sense of culture : Cross-cultural expeditions and management practices of self-initiated expatriates in the foreign workplace / Norhayati Zakaria.
Description: Boca Raton : Taylor & Francis, 2019. | Includes bibliographical references and index.
Identifiers: LCCN 2019002002 (print) | LCCN 2019006511 (ebook) | ISBN 9781351034586 (e-Book) | ISBN 9781138490765 (hardback : alk. paper)
Subjects: LCSH: International business enterprises--Management--Social aspects. | Management--Cross-cultural studies.
Classification: LCC HD62.4 (ebook) | LCC HD62.4 .N67 2019 (print) | DDC 658.3008--dc23
LC record available at https://lccn.loc.gov/2019002002

Contents

SECTION II   Cultural Impacts on Management Practices

SECTION III In Search of Global Talents with Cultural Intelligence

Foreword

Dr. Norhayati Zakaria and I have been doing a global dance together for almost a decade. Imagine us as two whirling dervishes, traveling at breakneck speed to do, act, experience, understand and instruct and then repeat the cycle over and over – trying to make individual and mutual sense of the cultural realities we are living through personally, as well as studying as our profession. We share a great passion for cultural engagement, as well as learning to how to live and operate in the world with great respect and compassion and transmitting this to others.

We believe in the work embodied in this book, as it has helped countless numbers of our students and colleagues to better interpret and, more importantly, act, to leave a positive mark on their world, not a trail of cultural misunderstanding and hurt feelings with global reach. Never has this material been more profoundly important for our planet's evolution as a global community. Thus, I was thrilled to be asked by "Dr. Yati," as she is known by her beloved students worldwide, to write a forward to her latest book. Her unique pathway for exploring both the challenges and promises of self-reflection on the cross-cultural journey, as well as models and experiments with behavioral adaptations, is a true gem for students and practitioners of cross-cultural communications alike.

As an American expatriate having traveled widely, as well as having lived in South America, the Middle East, Southeast Asia and Australia, I am keenly aware of how the interweaving of cultural complexity can lead to very unexpected outcomes, some charmingly delightful and some with disastrous consequences. As the world becomes more global, the blending of cultures does not get easier to navigate, but instead the complexities resulting from the interweaving become harder to interpret. As Dr. Yati so aptly points out in her Dubai "Global Village" example, even as we seem to be homogenizing on the surface – through social media, consumerism, and blending of values – the challenges of the new mix may be even more difficult to transcend than the former era, where a traveler visited a second culture and attempted to navigate differences between their home culture and that of the "other." From personal experience living in Dubai, I can attest to the fact that one might engage with a dozen or more "cultures" in the course of a work day. Never has the ability to navigate cultural complexity been more needed. Dr. Yati and I are united in our desire to support cross-cultural understandings, particularly through the training of our university students to negotiate these complexities, in order to create best-case outcomes for the multicultural communities in which they increasingly find themselves. She is apt in her observations that the best pathway forward is to impart reflective, flexible and adaptable skills to those motivated to navigate the challenges they face in the "new world."

This book, which, if written 10–15 years ago, would have been applicable to a thin slice of expatriate community, now has wide-reaching import to a global audience grappling with cross-cultural understandings big and small. This new book captures the enthusiasm and creativity that Dr. Yati brings to her teaching, through the use of rich vignettes that authentically capture many of the common interpretive challenges experienced by expats working in such cultures. I applaud her efforts to encapsulate these experiences through the voices of her students and transmit them to a new generation of expatriates struggling with the timeless challenges of navigating different cultures. Having taught beside Dr. Yati in Dubai for three years, I have been a direct observer of her capacities to transmit this skill to students from all walks of life, as well as to create the kinds of trusting, transparent relationships required to mutually navigate the complexities of the intensely multicultural work and social contexts found in a "salad bowl" like Dubai.

I am confident educators and trainers focused on diversity and cross-cultural communications will appreciate this book's rich and authentic representations of real-life struggles with this material. There are many lessons to be learned from our inveterate cultural guru. Those fortunate enough to have picked up this book will surely be delighted by the insights they gain from these pages, as well as the power it holds to influence their ability to engage more productively in the wider world. I hope your engagement with Dr. Yati's work is as rich and fulfilling as it has been for those of us privileged enough to encounter her on her globetrotting adventures.

Jenny Knowles Morrison, PhD
Research Fellow
Lyndon B. Johnson School of Public Affairs
The University of Texas at Austin
Jenny.knowles.morrison@utexas.edu

Prelude

To undergo a cross-cultural journey, means to grapple with multidimensional cultural frontiers and obstructions. With such perplexing twists and unknowns turns, expatriates are bound to connect the dots through cultural sensemaking.

Norhayati Zakaria

I lived and studied in the United States as an expatriate for eight years, during which I discovered cultural intricacies that were far, deep and wide ranging. Indeed, these years of exploring the sea of cultural opportunities and oddities equipped me with invaluable cross-cultural competency. Thereafter, I was truly blessed to fulfil my dream of becoming an academic expatriate when I first entered Dubai in 2009 on a seconded, or assigned, basis. After a few years, as per my contractual agreement with my former university. I returned to my home country of Malaysia with a new cultural outlook. However, in 2016, after extensive debate with my family members and numerous predicaments such as leaving my old-age parents, siblings and close friends, job security, accustomed lifestyles and familiar surroundings, I re-entered Dubai as a self-initiated expatriate (SIE) with the aspiration of becoming a global academician; I hoped to embark on cross-cultural expeditions around the world with a view to exploring and acquiring culturally oriented experiences, knowledge and wisdom.

Following my return to Dubai, the first six months constituted an extended "honeymoon period." Undeniably, I could still vividly remember how excited I was when I first came to Dubai. Why? Well, why *not*? The most plausible answer to this question is that spending three consecutive years in Dubai from 2009–2012 indeed groomed, attuned and educated me with regard to the expected cycle of culture shock and its nuances. Consequently, the second time around, the culture-shock stage appeared to come much later in the adjustment process. Lysgaard (1955) affirmed through his U-curve adjustment theory that expatriates might take between nine months and four years to fully adjust to life in the host country and eventually achieve cultural mastery. True enough, when I re-entered Dubai, I was filled with bliss because I was already familiar with the country, my colleagues and the workplace systems, routines and procedures. I also found the social environment enjoyable. In short, I felt that I knew it all! Unfortunately, over time (i.e., in just over six months), I began to experience the cultural adjustment challenges again, undergoing cycles of culture shock, which were accompanied by a certain degree of distress and unpleasantness. Only then did it dawn on me that culture is both complex and mysterious. One cannot and should not be too content with understanding the known effects of culture, given its multifaceted factors – that is, one's interactions, as well as one's general living and working conditions. People differ, and their behaviours such as tolerance for power disparity vs. empowerment, time-urgency vs. time-delayed, risk taker vs. risk averse, individualism vs. collectivism, relationship orientation vs. task orientation and many others can be mind blowing if these cultural differences are not well understood and communicated among colleagues.

As an expatriate, sojourner and traveller, I have had amazing global experiences, braving numerous years of cross-cultural expeditions in a foreign country. I have discovered that it is only through a deep sense of realization that one is able to make sense of culture. The following are key questions that should be considered by all SIEs who are willing to undertake the process of expatriation: Why and when shall I engage in cultural reflection? Moreover, how do I make sense of culture?

Without doubt, cultural sensemaking is not only a process but also a tool for knowing oneself and others. Expatriates need to take the plunge and have the courage to explore the numerous oddities and possibilities that are associated with living abroad. Without fail, such sacrifices of being abroad and global experiences have taught me an abundance of lessons. Consequently, I have grown from a naïve and culturally unsavvy individual into a culturally mature one. In fact, I have become a culturally savvy academician who is passionate about cultural intelligence with regard to the analysis of organizational behaviour. As the years came to pass, I faced many surprising incidents that had either unintended or intended consequences. For example, I started contemplating the answers to the questions that a colleague whispered to me: "Why didn't you say something in the meeting just now about the issue that seemed to bother you last week?" and "Why didn't you say no and refuse to do the task that was shoved on to you unexpectedly?" These are among the many mystifying issues that allow others to observe and scrutinize our cultural norms, attitudes, beliefs and actions. Making sense of culture is not as easy as I thought it would be, and, apparently, making sense of the *self* against the backdrop of culture is even more perplexing; this is because your understanding of the *self* can be inaccurate and unrealistic in the eyes of others. You could be a victim of cultural unknowns and peculiarities. For example, with a frown on her face, Emilie asked me, "Why did you refer to your parents about your choice of work? Isn't that a personal choice and a decision exclusively to be made by an individual?" Or, "Why did you seek permission from your husband when you wanted to leave the house?" A stranger or colleague could continuously question your attitudes, beliefs and cultural values because he or she is clueless about the underlying assumptions that underpin the truth of cultural justifications.

As an SIE, my cross-cultural experiences have revealed the meanings of culture and have validated its truth by unpacking numerous culturally perplexing behaviours. Unquestionably, and as I had anticipated, my journey has been fascinating, and through the lens of my Cross-Cultural Management classroom, I have scrutinized dozens of my own cross-cultural reflections, all of which have been rooted in my attitudes, values, perceptions and behaviours. Based on these reflections, I created a blog called "Cross-Cultural Expeditions." It was refreshing and insightful to observe and learn about the myriad amazing experiences shared by my postgraduate students and myself based on one intriguing question: What is it like to experience the forces and effects of culture in the workplace as an expatriate? After years of reflecting on my maiden cross-cultural journey as an academic expatriate, I decided to make sense of the shared experiences of expatriation. Thus, this book was developed based on the 10 weeks of blogs on culturally oriented narrations about myself and others as SIEs. It was after analyzing these 10 weeks of blogs that I realized how challenging it was to dissect, unpack and discover the powerful effects of culture on human behaviour at work and in life more generally. Nonetheless, the experience of immersing myself completely in cultural sensemaking has been an enriching journey of discovering myself and others.

In a nutshell, I strongly advocate that unless and until we acknowledge that culture is the essence of humankind and that it shapes people with its magical touches of diversity and uniqueness, the global world will fail to view people inclusively and embrace tolerance, appreciation and happiness! At the beginning of 2019, His Highness Sheikh Mohammed bin Rashid Al Maktoum, the ruler of Dubai, proudly and respectfully designated 2019 as *The Year of Tolerance*, using the national tree called *Ghaf* as a logo that symbolizes the principles of tolerance, coexistence and diversity. Indeed, through cultural sensemaking, the ultimate reflective practices unite people from diverse cultures, encouraging them to embrace tolerance at all costs and at all levels, as everyone who populates Dubai's multicultural society should focus on the seven pillars of tolerance, which are Islam as a religion, the UAE's Constitution, Zayed's legacy and ethics of the UAE, international conventions, archaeology and history, humanity and common values. Cultural incongruities are real, and making sense of them can be complex; consequently, people are compelled to have a high measure of tolerance.

Norhayati Zakaria
University of Wollongong in Dubai
December 15, 2018

Acknowledgments

The fruition of this long-awaited book would not be possible without the strength bestowed to me by the Gracious Almighty. This book wouldn't have become a reality without the collaborative efforts of cultural sensemaking between my postgraduate students (cohort of 2010) and myself. Hence, to the expatriates in the classes, I would like to appropriately pen a thank-you note to all 60 of my former students to fully acknowledge their cultural aspirations. I firmly believe that they have become what I call culturally savvy managers. If and when they pick up this book, I want them to know that they made it to the finishing line as cultural intellectuals because they began with inquisitive minds that provoked their cultural awareness and inculcated their sensitivity to cultural differences. I then witnessed them grow into people with different culturally tuned mindsets, affections and actions. Please note that to protect the confidentiality of the respondents in this research, all names of the people who responded to the blogs will remain unknown and private since I have used fictitious names to represent the different nationalities, which depicts the uniqueness of the cultural encounters and experiences of each of them. Only their insightful opinions, rich experiences and enlightening expressions given in the blogs were used to illustrate incidences or practices of relevance.

To the other people in my life who have made this book worth the patience and time, I wish to thank my pillar of strength and supportive soulmate – Dr. Shafiz Affendi Mohd Yusof; my loving parents (Zakaria Othman and Taburiah Ali) and in-laws (Mohd Yusof Hasan and Fatimah Saad), who continuously granted me their prayers, blessing and support from afar for the many missing years; my seven loving siblings who enjoyed listening to my cultural nuances, joys and pains; my multiple editors who relentlessly read the many incomplete drafts at a distance over the years; my colleagues and siblings, Dr. Jenny Knowles, Andrea Amelinckx, J.D., Dr. Sharipah Soa'ad, Dr. Norsaadah Zakaria and Dr. Nasriah Zakaria, who have diligently read several chapters that needed a sharp eye, with persuasive articulation; and my editorial administrator, Nursakirah Ab Rahman Muton, who has diligently assisted me with the formatting and developing visual graphics. To the managing editors of Routledge, in particular Kristine Mednansky, Katherine Kadian, Jennifer Stair and

Victoria Burns, thank you for the patience and cooperation to support the birth of this book. Without these people, and without this cultural expedition, it would not have been possible for me to grow as a person who sees things with high cultural indebtedness and not as a person with a cultural blind spot.

Author

Dr. Norhayati Zakaria is an associate professor at the University of Wollongong in Dubai and she teaches undergraduate courses such as responsible leadership, managing across cultures, integrated business capstone, and postgraduate courses such as research project for human resource management, and managerial skills and concepts. She graduated from the School of Information Studies at Syracuse University. She obtained her PhD in Information Science and Technology and MPhil in Information Transfer. She also obtained her MS (Management) from Rensselaer Polytechnic Institute, Troy, New York and BBA (Human Resource Management) from Universiti Utara Malaysia. Her educational training bridges several interdisciplinary fields: cross-cultural management, international business, international human resource management, and information system.

Dr. Zakaria's research program aims at exploring on how and why cultural values shape people differently in terms of communication styles, leadership, global virtual and team dynamics, and management practices like decision-making approaches and negotiation patterns. Specifically, she is interested in further exploring the research agenda with a key question of: what are the cross-cultural kits needed for globally-talented human resources to build cross-culturally-competent individuals and how do they develop culturally-versatile competency and technologically savvy skills to effectively perform in the novelty virtual work structure such as global virtual teams. Her first monograph entitled *Culture Matters: Decision Making of Global Virtual Teams* marked her scholarly work in the area of research that integrates cross-cultural management and information science fields relevantly. She is also building another research agenda pertaining to "Self-Initiated Expatriates" which led to her second monograph entitled: *Making Sense of Culture: Cross-Cultural Expeditions and Management Practices of Self-Initiated Expatriates in the Foreign Workplace.* This book provides a significant pathway for her to strive on the research agenda by exploring the influence of cultural values on expatriation processes given their encounters of managerial practices, relocation processes and challenges, and the sacrifices made by individuals and their families as a social-cultural support system.

For more than a decade, she has established international research collaborations with global scholars from the United States, Japan, the United Arab Emirates, South Africa, and Canada. She has secured international grant as the Principal Investigator from organizations like Asian Office of Aerospace Research Development (AOARD) as well as Co-Investigators from funding grants like Japanese Society for the Promotion of Sciences, Nippon Foundation, Fundamental Research Grant Scheme (Ministry of Higher Education Malaysia), and National Science Foundation. Some of her selected publications are indexed by ABDC, ISI, or Scopus such as Academy of Management and Learning Education, Journal of International Management, International Journal of Manpower, IT and People, the Database for Advances in Information System, and Creativity and Innovation Management.

Section I

Understanding Culture and Self-Initiated Expatriates

1

Making Sense of Culture

One could be at the crossroads of culture, one could fear the uncertainty, but one will never lose one's sense of culture, as long as one relentlessly make sense of culture!

Norhayati Zakaria

BLOG VIGNETTE 1.1   How It First Begins:
Life as a Self-Initiated Expatriate

Looking back, I remember that from childhood to adolescence I spent my time obsessively watching movies from different cultures – American, English, Arabian, Chinese, Indian and Indonesian. What I remember most vividly is that I was mesmerized by the intricacy of behaviours which were so different from my own and those of everyone I knew. For example, in the 1980s, when I watched my all-time favourite American family dramas, such as *Eight is Enough, Family Ties* or *Little House on the Prairie*, I learned so much about family values which, in terms of independence, relationships and communication, were unique and distinct from my own Asian values. Rather than intimidating me, such differences enticed me to learn more about my own roots and values. At the time, I could only absorb all of this information, not yet knowing where or how to apply such culturally oriented knowledge in my daily life. Undoubtedly this early exposure created in me a strong sense of cultural awareness and invoked a cultural sensitivity that eventually led me to become a culturally intelligent and savvy academician. The observation of myriad behaviours from different backgrounds gave me an appreciation of various ways of doing things. Ever since I was exposed to foreign lands through my television, I wanted to travel. I have always wanted to see worlds other than my own. I was intensely curious about how others live their lives and why people behave differently. Indeed, up until now, I have travelled the world, from West to East, North to South, and almost all the continents in the world to savour the cultural nuances. I wanted to explore people's minds, emotions and actions and the impacts of these on the way people live their daily lives as well as how they behave in the workplace.

CULTURAL LESSONS 1.1: THE JOURNEY OF EXPLORING THE MULTITUDES OF CULTURE

In the fall of 2009, I moved from Malaysia to Dubai full of enthusiasm and eagerness. I had accepted a job offer as an assistant professor for the Faculty of Business and Management at a premier Australian university in Dubai. I had been teaching for almost 13 years at a local university before I plunged into the decision to work abroad, and thus I stamped my passport for the global path of my career! It was the same decision I had made a decade earlier when I became a student expatriate in the United States, where I lived and was educated for almost eight years. Many people have asked me, "Why did you move?" and "What made you stay overseas that long?" Or, to put it in more technical terms, why did I become a self-initiated expatriate (SIE) – first as a student and then as an academician?

As I begin to build my research program, my field of research expertise combines several multidisciplinary fields, cross-cultural management, international human resource management and international business, with a fundamental concept called "culture" that connects all the diverse disciplines. More than a decade ago, I began to craft my research on culturally oriented organizational behaviours, also known as cross-cultural management. In the spring of 2010, I taught a 10-week course on cross-cultural management to postgraduate students. Through this course, I sought to explore and discover the influence of culture in the workplace and the dynamic role it plays when people of different cultural backgrounds work together. I blogged regularly about the challenges I faced in Dubai during my early months there to make sense of my own cultural challenges through reflection. I also wanted to introduce a series of reflections on cross-cultural experience – stories which were narrated by my students, who were also primarily SIEs if not organizational-based expatriates. The stories would be a blend of the "sweet and sour" moments of living and working in a foreign land as an SIE. On a weekly basis, I asked the students to discuss their cultural encounters and cultural insights, both at work and in their personal lives.

One of the assignments required the students to reflect deeply on their thoughts, values, attitudes and behaviours – what they were doing, had done and would do – based on their own cultural values. The journey of recognizing their cultural sensemaking thus demanded that the students be very sensitive to and aware of their thoughts, feelings and actions. My goal for the 10-week course was not only to shape each of them into a competent global manager but also to help them become culturally intelligent. I believed that a blog would be the perfect platform for sharing the many interesting personal and professional stories relating to how culture affects organizational behaviours. I also looked forward to receiving as many stories as possible from students from all walks of life.

Workplace ambiance is an important cultural dimension that can help us in understanding how we work and what kind of working environment we prefer. My main motto and short answer is this: keep smiling – it might make someone's day! Recollecting the first class session, I was starting my old course in a new semester and a new location. I called it an old course because I had taught it previously in Malaysia, having been a cross-cultural management teacher for more than a decade. I chose this course because it was where my passions lay. Every semester I vowed to try a different approach to the class, and sure enough, every semester I found new ways to stimulate the cross-cultural discussions that formed a key part of the course. That spring of 2010, as I entered the classroom at six in the evening, I looked at my potential students with eagerness and a bit of anxiety. They looked at me with frowns and worried expressions … no smiles greeted me. Not knowing what to expect from one another made us greet each other with serious faces. I should have done better; if I was too serious, they would be, too. As the class went on, the frowns began to intensify to expressions of worry, especially after I reviewed the tasks to be completed for the course. I saw jaws drop, heard questions of "What?" and noticed a few ugly looks on faces around the room when they learned that the class would require four assignments.

As an educator, it is not a pleasure to make people do too many things or work excessively hard. But as a teacher who is experienced in the field, I find that when I provide multiple assignments, students grow to appreciate critical reflections. Consequently, such an ability creates wonders for knowledge fulfilment. I had hoped that my class would benefit from such training as I could offer. My own training during my years in the United States involved rigorous work, where I was required to manage and complete many tasks that, in the end, shaped me to be a critical thinker. I had to fight my way up. My professors in graduate school used to give miniature assignments on a weekly basis; this drained us students, but the outcome was miraculous as we finished the program, be it a Masters or PhD. My educational background shaped me as a teacher. It moulded my educational culture, so to speak. So, that day, after I finished explaining the tasks to my students, there was relief in my heart as I saw people begin to nod and smile. A smile at the end of a session is a positive clue; it says, "Okay, I understand what is needed." But there was the other half of the class that just shook their heads, releasing sighs that I could hear from afar. What did that mean? Okay, or not okay? I explained that each of them needed to think over the demands of the class and continue with the course only if they had the passion and strength to undertake the challenge. There was no pressure on them to do so since the course was an elective – they could stay or go; it was purely their own choice.

I have always wanted my students to understand the reasons behind each assignment. One bright student asked me at the end of that first session,

"What do you want us to achieve in this class?" This was a wonderful question because it gave me a chance to explain the benefits of the course. I said that I hoped they would achieve three things: become culturally competent by cultivating an awareness of cultural differences, develop an emotional tolerance for and appreciation of those differences and – the toughest of all – reshape their behaviours to be more flexible so that they could accept cultural differences and act accordingly. Three simple outcomes, but before them lay many obstacles, as we were dealing with the intricacies of human behaviour. My ultimate desire was to inculcate a passion for culture in the students as the global manager to-be, to further their – and my own – understanding of the powerful effect of culture on behaviour and, most importantly, to uncover how cultural roots manifest themselves in the many forms of behaviour in the workplace.

A ROADMAP OF CULTURAL EXPEDITION OF SELF-INITIATED EXPATRIATES

The topic of this book lies at the intersection of three interdisciplinary fields which are crucial to bridge in the modern and global business environment: cross-cultural management, international human resource management and international business. The consequences of globalization have led to a more extensive recruitment process as companies seek people of global talents to fit the different work structures and competitive work environment of tomorrow. The growing number of SIEs further intensifies the challenges faced by multinational organizations because people searching for better career prospects are increasingly willing to relocate in order to obtain competitive salaries or compensation packages – or, like myself, to experience the pleasure of a new country. Multinational corporations need to acknowledge the influence of culture on management practices because these expatriates will bring their own cultural attitudes and uniqueness to their new company. By integrating the two fields mentioned above, I hope this book will be a valuable guide to SIEs, enhancing their understanding of the richness of cultural behaviours and the challenges and potential rewards of a global cultural workplace. This book is also developed to train people to effectively manage people across cultures and ultimately become cross-culturally intelligent leaders, managers and teams.

With the goal in mind of developing culturally competent SIEs, this book is organized into 10 chapters with three main parts. The first part: *Understanding Culture and SIEs*, introduces the phenomenon and definition of SIEs and key cultural concepts, dimensions and theories. Chapter 1 introduces the reader to my experience as an SIE and the structure of the book in order to provide a road map on what to expect from the book. Chapter 2 expands on the definition of culture and its many layers, which give rise to complexities in the international workplace. This chapter also introduces cross-cultural theories, which advances the field of cross-cultural management and international business from the late 1970s–1990s based on reputable theorists – Hall (1976), Hofstede (1984) and Trompenaars and Hampden-Turner (1997). Chapter 3 presents an overview of the expatriation process, what it takes to be an expatriate and the repatriation process. It is important for any SIE to develop high self-awareness based on the four different stages as they undergo the volatility of cross-cultural adjustment cycles. Chapter 4 examines the power of reflection for SIEs when they undergo the journey of cross-cultural adjustments. Inherently, the need for the cultural sensemaking process via reflection approaches for expatriates who aim to be successful during their expatriation process is crucial. This chapter also outlines the value and need for reflection and the process by which an expatriate can effectively reflect and undergo cultural sensemaking. The two guided models of reflection are the onion model (Hofstede, 1984) and cycle of reflection model (Gibbs, 1988).

The second part is *Cultural Impacts on Management Practices*, comprising Chapters 5 through 8 in which I will provide an understanding of the impacts of culture on management practices. Specifically, in Chapter 5, I explore the importance of understanding how communication is approached differently by people from different cultures. Communication is the essence of collaboration in the workplace. It is the glue that binds a relationship and creates a bridge between people to promote effective performance. In Chapter 6, I look at a second element that is required for people to work together: negotiation. Yet, what is challenging for a cross-cultural negotiation process is the ways and means of negotiation which is different based on the culture. Negotiation is a process in which people present their opinions and ideas, then discuss and debate them to determine the best outcome. Chapter 7 discusses the challenges surrounding decision-making when people of different cultures have different ways of negotiating and communicating their decisions. Who makes decisions, when decisions take place, and how are they made, are some of the key questions to reflect on by global managers. Culture affects the entire decision-making process.

Likewise, trust and its boundary in terms of private and public space is also an important element that affects how people make decisions in different cultures. Chapter 8 further examines culture and leadership styles from the viewpoint of hierarchy vs. empowerment and their attitudes towards equality and inequality. It is important to note that organizational structure that is tall, that is, pyramid-like, exemplifies a culture that promotes inequality in power distribution, and such a condition is well accepted by the society, which illustrates, "You are the Boss, and I am obliged to follow as guided and instructed." On the other hand, in a culture which has a flat structure, it emphasizes empowerment that clearly delineates the following aspect: "Although I am the boss, we can discuss what needs to be done."

The third part is *In Search of Global Talents with Cultural Intelligence*, where the book will wrap up with the two closing chapters. In Chapter 9, I will highlight the meaning of cultural intelligence and present the development of such intelligence using the CAB model of cross-cultural competencies, which are based on cognitive, affective and behavioural skills. It is important for SIEs to achieve cultural competencies and become culturally fit and intelligent people when they are working abroad. The final chapter will provide a conclusion on how SIEs can cross cultural boundaries and effectively move forward by revisiting several checklists on how to become culturally competent.

The structure of the book is that each chapter will be composed of five main sections – *blog vignettes, cultural lessons, case blogs, cultural reflections, and cultural ponders* (the details as outlined in the roadmap; refer to Figure 1.1). Throughout the book, it will consist of blog entries, vignettes, and mini case studies that depict culture in action in the daily workplace in people's perceptions, attitudes, values and norms. Each chapter is based on a story; taken together, they follow the trajectory of what I experienced during the early stages of being an SIE in both my career and my daily life as an academician in a foreign land. The voices in the book are reflective of my own mind as well as other students who responded to my questions and shared their stories on my blog. At the end of each chapter are illustrative cases that support the topic or theme to help the reader further appreciate and gain insight into culturally influenced scenarios in the workplace. Each chapter offers key questions to stimulate critical reflection and encourage the reader to apply what has just been read. At the end of every chapter, I will provide cultural ponders as reflective scenarios illustrated by my blog respondents to demonstrate their own interpretations of cultural influence on the management practices during their SIE's experience.

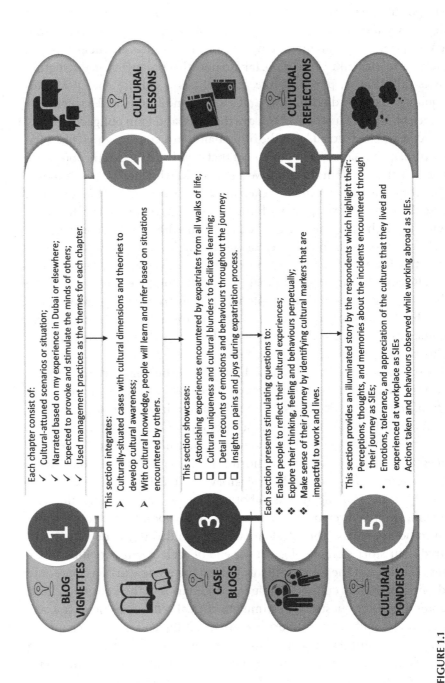

BLOG VIGNETTES

1

Each chapter consist of:
- ✓ Cultural-attuned scenarios or situation;
- ✓ Narrated based on my experience in Dubai or elsewhere;
- ✓ Expected to provoke and stimulate the minds of others;
- ✓ Used management practices as the themes for each chapter.

2

CULTURAL LESSONS

This section integrates:
- ⋏ Culturally-situated cases with cultural dimensions and theories to develop cultural awareness;
- ⋏ With cultural knowledge, people will learn and infer based on situations encountered by others.

CASE BLOGS

3

This section showcases:
- ❑ Astonishing experiences encountered by expatriates from all walks of life;
- ❑ Cultural uniqueness and cultural blunders to facilitate learning;
- ❑ Detail recounts of emotions and behaviours throughout the journey;
- ❑ Insights on pains and joys during expatriation process.

4

CULTURAL REFLECTIONS

Each section presents stimulating questions to:
- ❖ Enable people to reflect their cultural experiences;
- ❖ Explore their thinking, feeling and behaviours perpetually;
- ❖ Make sense of their journey by identifying cultural markers that are impactful to work and lives.

CULTURAL PONDERS

5

This section provides an illuminated story by the respondents which highlight their:
- • Perceptions, thoughts, and memories about the incidents encountered through their journey as SIEs;
- • Emotions, tolerance, and appreciation of the cultures that they lived and experienced at workplace as SIEs
- • Actions taken and behaviours observed while working abroad as SIEs.

FIGURE 1.1

The book roadmap to explore cross-cultural expeditions of self-initiated expatriates.

1.1 @CULTURAL PONDERS

Even When You Travel, Culture Shock Is Real and Still Exists!

Yusof Al Barak

Autumn 2010

Sometimes it is really difficult for us to cope in a place other than home. I personally wouldn't be able to migrate to another country. This is due to my strong relationship with my family and the sense that I need to be around them. Being a UAE national, and coming from a Muslim religion, we truly hold onto our families, and family relationship really means a lot to us. Of course, I travel abroad for holiday purposes which may not last more than 2–4 weeks usually. I get culture shock and I start feeling alienated, like a stranger in the country, when travelling to a new place. I even regret that I have travelled until I get used to the place and know my way around. One model that is helpful for understanding culture shock when we encounter travelling issues is the iceberg model. We know that an iceberg has only 10% of its total mass above the water while 90% of it is underwater. But that 90% is what the ocean currents act on and what creates the iceberg's behaviour at its tip. Cultural understanding can be looked at in this same way. An example of the iceberg model can be seen in our own health. Catching a cold is an event, and if we continue to catch a cold more frequently and feel tired, then there is a pattern. The systemic structures or causes for getting tired might include overwork, unhealthy diet or insufficient rest. We tend to get lost in the immediate event of suffering from a cold, forgetting that it is part of a pattern of events that is caused by the underlying structures of our lifestyle. If we take a "system-thinking" approach to solving the problem of frequent colds, we would try to find ways to make ourselves less overtired, rather than just focusing on the immediate relief (in the form of aspirin or other medicine) that solves the problem of the current cold. So, basically, when we move to a new country, either migrating, working or even for travelling purposes, we cannot adapt in the first instance since our tradition, beliefs, values and culture are entirely different. Until we deepen our knowledge and try to understand the things around us that makes us feel more comfortable or uncomfortable, we will continue to resist changes and thus undergo culture shock and hence will likely fail to acculturate in the end. In my case, nonetheless, I will still feel homesick, and I will still be reluctant to move abroad, because I cannot envision myself as an expatriate at this moment!

2

Defining Culture

A people without the knowledge of their past history, origin and culture is like a tree without roots.

Marcus Garvey

BLOG VIGNETTE 2.1   Cultural Nuances in the Workplace

"Take it easy. Be cool," Eldana Ibraimova told herself on the way to the office that morning, trying to calm down as she remembered yesterday evening's event. The Kazakhstan native had been overjoyed when she moved to Dubai two years previously to work as an expatriate in a global manufacturing firm. As sad as she had been to leave her parents and friends back home, she had never looked back – at least not until yesterday. It had happened at 6 p.m. as she was preparing to leave the office to go home. Her managing director from Australia confronted her forcefully. "Eldana, can you please tell me what was in the deal that you negotiated with our client in South Africa?" she asked. "Mr. Orumsawe called me and was very angry because he said you didn't provide the right marketing campaign for our new project there. He was upset. This issue needs to be dealt with immediately!" The manager then walked away. Eldana was astounded and felt numb. For the past two years, she had been very efficient with her overseas clients and no one had complained or disliked her work. "Something's not right," she thought as she tried to gauge what was the matter. "Is the problem the way my manager spoke to me, or is the problem that she is implying I have been slacking?" Either way, she was perplexed at her manager's actions.

The above illustration is an example of one of the many nuanced cultural interactions that can occur within the workplace. Cultural challenges can come in many forms, at any moment in your daily routine and with anyone you interact with, whether you know them or not. Although these interactions can be painful, frustrating and confusing, nevertheless, they offer the dynamism and richness of experiencing a culture that is different from your own values, beliefs, attitudes and perceptions. As such, cultural interactions will continuously stimulate and challenge your mindset, attitudes and tolerance as well as motivating your actions and behaviours to search for the right way to deal with the cultural idiosyncrasies and complexity of behaviours.

Culture has a powerful way of demonstrating one's true self and revealing the mysteries of others. The way a person speaks, how one expresses oneself and the approaches a person employs indicate one's culture. For example, in Eastern cultures, when people are faced with conflict with someone else, they do not confront the other person directly. Instead, they prefer to ask someone else to approach the person or use a mediated platform to express the situation.

When they speak, they use an indirect manner to express the conflicting situation, carefully wording the issue to avoid exacerbating the situation. In contrast, Westerners speak directly to the person in a confrontational manner in order to solve a problem. What is important is to solve the disagreement quickly, since people consider tasks to take precedence over relationships. Such a different approach and style of communication is rooted in the way a person was brought up. Hence, the more you know about yourself, the more you will recognize your strengths as well as your insufficiencies.

In the age of globalization, people are experiencing the world as a borderless structure where knowledge transfer is freely disseminated across the globe. Information technology and social communication media facilitate the transfer of cultural knowledge at a phenomenal rate. Expatriation has thus become a much easier process than it was decades ago, as people can now learn about other cultures before they decide to move to another country. With social networking sites such as Facebook, Instagram, Twitter and others, we can reach out and collaborate with people from different cultural backgrounds more intensely.

Therefore, a difficulty that arises in the work environment is cooperating with people who have different work natures, beliefs and practices – which consequently leads to some unexpected challenges. To understand these challenges, we must first understand the meaning of culture. So, what is culture actually? Can we define this concept so that those who decide to become expatriates can learn to manage its complexities in the global workplace? Expatriates are not the only ones who need to understand the meaning and effects of culture; managers and organizations also need to be aware, practice tolerance and apply appropriate strategies for managing expatriates to create high-performing organizational teams.

CULTURAL LESSON 2.1: WHAT IS CULTURE?

Mahatma Gandhi argued that culture comes from the soul and resides in the heart of a person. In contrast, Hofstede (1991) viewed culture as one's mental programming – a software of the mind. He proposed three levels of mental programming that differ from one another in terms of their characteristics and nature. First was the concept of personality. In the field of psychology, people develop their personalities from childhood and throughout their lifetimes. Such development and learning processes take place at the individual level.

At the same time, people can also be influenced by the internal and external environments in which they grow up – their family, school and community/society. In this combined environment, groups influence how a person will behave in their growing years until adulthood – in life and the workplace.

When a person's values, attitudes, beliefs, practices and norms are affected by the group environment, these then become cultural values. Cultural values affect a person at the group level, where the culture belongs to a specific group or category. Members of a society behave in a similar way because of shared cultural values among the people in the group. To some extent, the effect of personality is less salient and dominant when culture affects a member in a group. Two renowned American anthropologists, Kroeber and Kluckhohn (1952, p. 181), penned this extensive definition of culture:

> [Culture] consists of patterns, explicit and implicit, of and for behavior acquired and transmitted by symbols, constituting the distinctive achievements of human groups, including their embodiment in artifacts; the essential core of culture consists of traditional ideas and especially their attached values; a culture system may, on the one hand, be considered as products of action, on the other, as conditional elements of future action.

In a similar vein, Schwartz (1992, p. 17) defined culture as "... The derivatives of experience, more or less organized, learned, or created by the individuals of the population including those images or encodements and their interpretations (meanings) transmitted from past generations, from contemporaries, or formed by individuals themselves."

In the field of cross-cultural management, it is clearly established that culture is an intricate concept composed of more than 160 different definitions with a diverse range of understanding among scholars. Due to its complex nature, organizations need to understand and appreciate the influence of culture in their multicultural workforces.

Last, let's explore the concept of human nature, which affects all people at a universal level. All people, regardless of their personality or culture, have the same basic needs. For example, the theory of hierarchy of needs by Abraham Maslow (1943) states that all people have the same base needs. The first level of needs is physiological and includes shelter, water, food and sleep.

Thus, in terms of workplace behaviour, at the second level of needs, all people will also seek conditions that allow them to work in a secure manner. Without these two levels of essential needs, human survival would be a challenge, as the essence of humanity would be constrained. When we look at these three key concepts – personality, culture and human needs – we realize

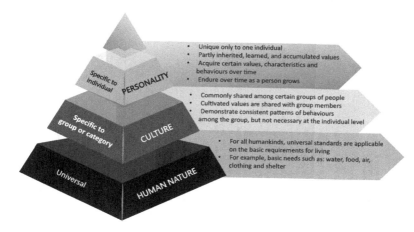

FIGURE 2.1
Layers of culture. (Adapted from Hofstede, G. 1991. *Cultures and Organizations: Software of the Mind*. London: McGraw-Hill.)

that culture is centred between two main concepts crucial to understanding human behaviours in the workplace (refer to Figure 2.1). It affects a person at the group level, where values are shared among people with common characteristics, such as country, organization, religion, gender, education, profession and so on. With different cultural layers, different expectations and preferences emerge and manifest in one's behaviours.

CULTURAL LESSON 2.2: HOW DOES CULTURE AFFECT YOU? RECOGNISING CULTURAL DIMENSIONS

As Kroeber and Kluckhohn (1952) explained, culture can be summarised as both observable and unobservable shared patterns of behaviour and values which permeate different contexts, environments and times. Cross-cultural management studies have examined the ways in which culture affects workplace behaviour and values. Likewise, international business studies have examined how culture influence business decisions and strategies. In both fields, three renowned cross-cultural theorists, Hall (1959, 1976), Hofstede (1984, 1991), and Trompenaars and Hampden-Turner (1997), have concluded that the complexity of culture lies in its various dimensions and provides underlying assumptions and theoretical explanations to key practical questions (see Figure 2.2). A total of 16 cultural dimensions were

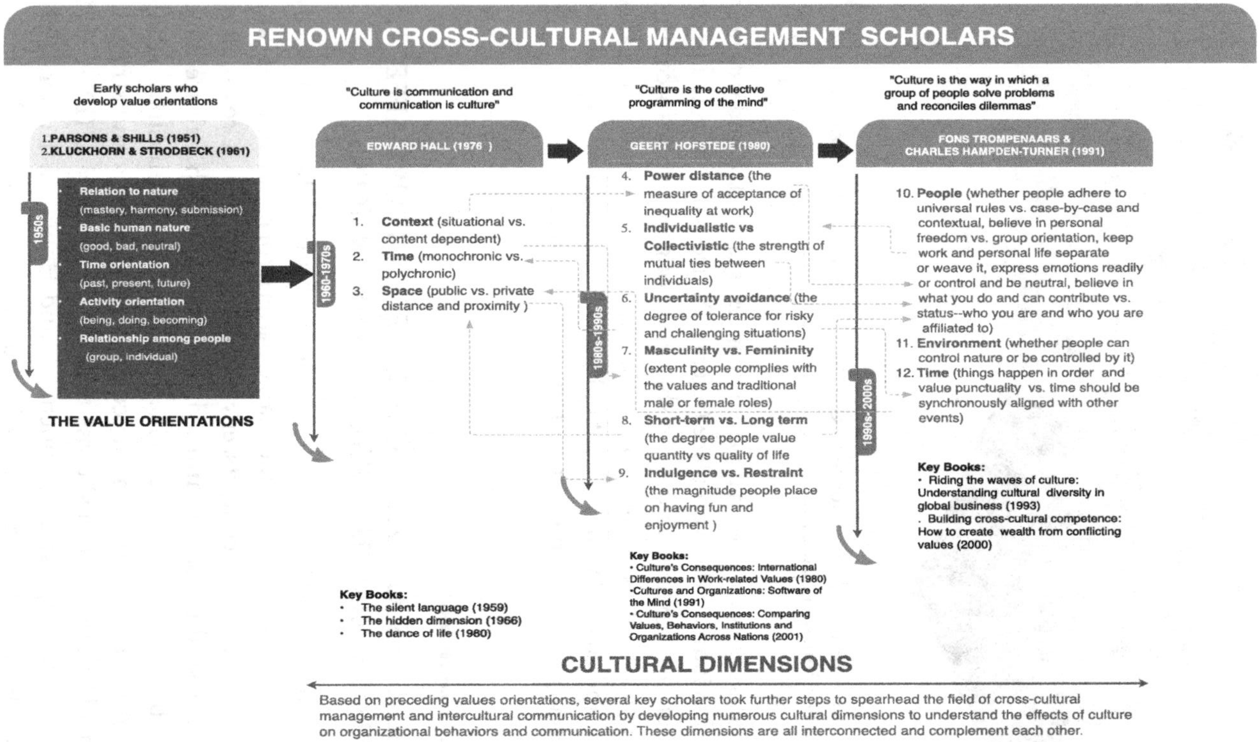

RENOWN CROSS-CULTURAL MANAGEMENT SCHOLARS

Early scholars who develop value orientations

1.PARSONS & SHILLS (1951)
2.KLUCKHORN & STRODBECK (1961)

THE VALUE ORIENTATIONS

Relation to nature (mastery, harmony, submission)

Basic human nature (good, bad, neutral)

Time orientation (past, present, future)

Activity orientation (being, doing, becoming)

Relationship among people (group, individual)

1950s

"Culture is communication and communication is culture"

EDWARD HALL (1976)

1. **Context** (situational vs. content dependent)
2. **Time** (monochronic vs. polychronic)
3. **Space** (public vs. private distance and proximity)

Key Books:
- The silent language (1959)
- The hidden dimension (1966)
- The dance of life (1980)

1960-1970s

"Culture is the collective programming of the mind"

GEERT HOFSTEDE (1980)

4. **Power distance** (the measure of acceptance of inequality at work)
5. **Individualistic vs Collectivistic** (the strength of mutual ties between individuals)
6. **Uncertainty avoidance** (the degree of tolerance for risky and challenging situations)
7. **Masculinity vs. Femininity** (extent people complies with the values and traditional male or female roles)
8. **Short-term vs. Long term** (the degree people value quantity vs quality of life
9. **Indulgence vs. Restraint** (the magnitude people place on having fun and enjoyment)

Key Books:
- Culture's Consequences: International Differences in Work-related Values (1980)
- Cultures and Organizations: Software of the Mind (1991)
- Culture's Consequences: Comparing Values, Behaviors, Institutions and Organizations Across Nations (2001)

1980s-1990s

"Culture is the way in which a group of people solve problems and reconciles dilemmas"

FONS TROMPENAARS & CHARLES HAMPDEN-TURNER (1991)

10. **People** (whether people adhere to universal rules vs. case-by-case and contextual, believe in personal freedom vs. group orientation, keep work and personal life separate or weave it, express emotions readily or control and be neutral, believe in what you do and can contribute vs. status--who you are and who you are affiliated to)
11. **Environment** (whether people can control nature or be controlled by it)
12. **Time** (things happen in order and value punctuality vs. time should be synchronously aligned with other events)

Key Books:
- Riding the waves of culture: Understanding cultural diversity in global business (1993)
- Building cross-cultural competence: How to create wealth from conflicting values (2000)

1990s- 2000s

CULTURAL DIMENSIONS

Based on preceding values orientations, several key scholars took further steps to spearhead the field of cross-cultural management and intercultural communication by developing numerous cultural dimensions to understand the effects of culture on organizational behaviors and communication. These dimensions are all interconnected and complement each other.

FIGURE 2.2

Cross-cultural theoretical framework by key scholars and development of cross-cultural dimensions.

developed by the abovementioned cross-cultural theorists. Over the past decades, worldwide researchers have employed these key cultural factors to understand its impacts on global businesses and to examine cultural influences on management practices.

Context, Time and Space

According to Hall (1959, 1976), three distinct cultural dimensions exist: context, time and space (see Table 2.1). My main premise is that the mannerisms, approaches and patterns of communicative behaviours are all contingent upon varied factors, such as the content of the message (examining the impact of culture on how messages are interpreted); who delivers and receives it; and why, when and how it is delivered. Answers to all of these questions provide meaning, as they rest upon two aspects – context (situation) and content (information). Hall argued that the meaning of information is embedded in a context to allow people to make sense of the message that is received. People deliver messages to communicate with others and then interpret the received messages based on the context.

Thus, context, meaning and information matter in communication, as they enable it to be effective, especially when it occurs between people from different cultures. In other words, context is crucial because it generates information, and a message is deemed meaningless if it has no context. Context is a continuum, along which meaning lies between two extreme points: high and low. The spectrum of meaning is embedded in a context which can be communicated using nonverbal zcues and/or verbal statements. In a high-context society, people value nonverbal cues more than verbal cues (written and spoken). High-context people look for nonverbal cues based on facial expressions, tone of voice, body language and hand gestures, all of which are conditional.

Conversely, people in a low-context culture need to express words explicitly for communication purposes because they cannot use implicitly shared information to a significant extent. Hence, they rely on content-dependent communication, which rests upon direct and explicit communication. The information needs to be crystallised and made explicit so that people can draw meaning from it. People in low-context cultures are keen to obtain the meaning of information based on textual statements and spoken words. They value information which is verbalised. Examples of countries that fall under the high-context umbrella are China, Japan, Thailand and India, while low-context countries include the United Kingdom, Canada and the United States (U.S.).

Hall also presents time and space as crucial dimensions that are related to high-context and low-context communication. There are two orientations of time: monochronic (M-time) and polychronic (P-time). People in a low-context culture belong to M-time, whereby time is viewed as being critical to the tasks to be undertaken. As such, people see time flows sequentially, tasks are conducted one at a time and have set deadlines, and punctuality is adhered to and respected. People in this context value adherence to an agenda in a meeting to ensure that tasks are aligned with what has carefully been planned and are based on schedules. M-time countries include the U.S., Scandinavian nations and Western European states. In P-time cultures, tasks can be carried out simultaneously, and people can engage in multitasking. Time is observed loosely, as reflected in attitudes such as flexible, relaxed, nonpunctual and nonurgent. Plans and agendas can be shifted, depending on people rather than on the business deals themselves. Countries that fall under the P-time umbrella include Southeast Asian, Latin American and African nations.

Another dimension indicated by Hall is space, which is also known as proxemics. It is an understanding of how people view nature and degree of space in different cultures. Moreover, the concept of proximity also enlightens us about the boundary of privacy and issues such as trust from the perspective of culture. It is important to take note that culture plays a role in what, why and how people develop trust over time. Boundaries are also bounded based on cultural values and beliefs. People have norms and rules prescribing what signifies private and public space between oneself and others like colleagues, friends and family members. Consequently, the following question arises: What is the boundary that people put between themselves when they relate to others in a social or interpersonal environment? Distances can be divided into four distinct zones: intimate, personal, social and public. Each zone prescribes different rules and guidelines regarding what, why, where and how people disclose information and how it carries different meanings in diverse cultures. The intimate zone is the close and personal bubble surrounding the space in which a person can get close to someone else, and it ranges from the touching zone to approximately two feet away. This space is normally occupied by people who share intimate relationships – certainly not by strangers. The personal zone is anywhere from two to four feet away, the social zone extends from four to twelve feet and the public zone is beyond twelve feet. Based on these descriptions of spatial zones, the way in which messages are communicated by people from different cultures depends on the levels of comfort of the individuals in question, the extent of their relationships, and the degree of trust they share. This raises the following question: How big is the personal bubble that you put between yourself and others? The answer is contingent upon whether you are dependent on content (information and text – that is, low-context culture) or context (situational and nonverbal cues – that is, high-context culture) – see the more detailed examples of the different aspects of context in Table 2.1.

Hierarchy, Close Ties, Risk, Achievement, Relationship and Gratification

In the late 1970s, cultural theorist Geert Hofstede conducted a survey of employees across the globe to examine the effects of national culture on behaviour in the organisational context. He collected the data by surveying thousands of executives at a leading multinational corporation – IBM – across 40 countries to understand their values and behaviours. He developed six dimensions of national culture based on an index: power distance, individualism vs. collectivism, uncertainty avoidance, masculinity vs. femininity, long term vs. short term, and indulgence vs. restraint (see Table 2.2).

First, the power distance dimension measures the level of acceptance of inequality in the distribution of power that exists among organisational members – that is, between top and lower management. It also informs the hierarchy that exists in the organisational structure and sets the boundary between people with a significant degree of status and power and those who have less of these. This dimension also illustrates how people perceive and distribute power and how they interpret and value authority. In a high power-distance culture, people accept an authority with power who provides instructions and makes final decisions. In contrast, a low power-distance culture readily empowers individuals to make their own decisions, people have lateral relationships with flattened structures, and relationships are not based on ranks within a hierarchical structure.

Second, the individualistic vs. collectivistic dimension informs the extent to which people are integrated into groups and to which they value self-expression over collective affiliation. This dimension also informs the level of ties between an individual and others; for example, people who value strong and tightly bound ties with others are more willing to work in groups and to take others' views into consideration. Contrastingly, people who have loose ties prefer independence and reliance on their immediate family members. They also prefer to express themselves using "I, me and myself," as opposed to "we, us and ourselves."

Third, the uncertainty avoidance dimension illustrates the level of tolerance for ambiguity. If there is a high level of uncertainty avoidance, the more ambiguous a situation, the more people will avoid risk taking. They prefer certainty and guided rules and approaches to ensure secure and reliable directions. However, when there is a low level of uncertainty avoidance, people prefer challenges and view risk taking as necessary for obtaining high returns on investment. They also value ideas and innovation; thus, less restrictive rules are imposed to promote innovative minds.

Fourth, the masculinity vs. femininity dimension measures success, which accounts for either achievement or quality of life. In a masculine culture, people prefer assertiveness, competitiveness and material rewards, and they look forward to attaining quantity in life. In this type of culture, members of society work hard to achieve their professional goals, and discrimination exists between genders. In a feminine culture, people prefer cooperation, caring and modesty; they subscribe to quality of life, and less distinction is made between men and women.

Fifth, this dimension relates to the time perspective, whether long- or short-term goals. In a long term–oriented society, people employ a frugal or thrifty attitude towards life when planning for the future, are pragmatic regarding how they plan, and persevere in terms of meeting goals and overcoming challenges. Their focus is centred on future orientation. In a short term–oriented society, people prefer to honour traditions and uphold culturally rooted rituals and customs which focus on their past cultural heritage. However, they also focus on the concept of "saving face" to protect established relationships. What has occurred in the past will become evident in the present if people do not protect the relationship that was developed; thus, taking care of people and connections is crucial.

Finally, the indulgence vs. restraint dimension relates to the degree to which people control their desires and impulses. An indulgent society normally values enjoyment. The members of this society feel that life offers numerous possibilities, that it has many aspects for which its members should be grateful, and that following human desires is acceptable and even necessary. Conversely, people who come from a restrained society make choices more carefully and in a more restricted fashion. They make decisions less freely, and gratification needs to be grounded and bound by strict rules and conditions. Hence, people in this culture sometimes fail to enjoy life as it is and place comparatively less importance on leisure and spending time with friends.

People, the Environment, and Time (PET) Framework

Organisational consultants Trompenaars and Hampden-Turner (1997) developed seven cultural dimensions that align with those of the cross-cultural theorists discussed above. Trompenaars began his research by acknowledging that people often face dilemmas in the workplace due to cultural challenges. These dilemmas are driven by three factors: people, environment and time (see Table 2.3). Cultural dilemmas, nonetheless, need to be resolved and then reconciled. Problem-solving in the workplace requires an understanding of how and why dilemmas take place, because culturally rooted problems occur when dealing with people from different cultures. Trompenaars and Hampden-Turner used the metaphor of the mirror to describe cultural dilemmas. They suggest that people can make sense of and reflect what and how they perceive a situation that is encountered when they see themselves reflected in others. This way, people can create a sense of cultural self-awareness, question occurrences and why they happen, and get in touch with their emotions regarding these incidents. Thereafter, they can begin analysing the cultures of others to enable them to evaluate situations. People obtain meaning in stages – that is, by identifying the problems before solutions can be found and implemented. For this reason, it is important to have a detailed understanding of the three aspects that drive cultural dilemmas.

First, most culturally rooted problems are largely caused by the behaviours of people from different cultures; this is known as *people orientation* and entails five key cultural dimensions. Making sense of behaviours is crucial to creating an awareness of cultural effects and their impacts on management practices. People who work for organisations need to adhere to the rules and policies that are stipulated. People in a universalist culture follow a set of rules, and behaviours are aligned to meet certain standards in terms of the procedures and systems that are in place at work. However, in particularist cultures, behaviours are conditioned and facilitated by the relationships that people develop with others over time. For instance, if a person has an established relationship with his or her boss, the rules can be "bent" – that is, made flexible – to suit the needs of this person. People are, therefore, treated on a case-by-case basis. However, in a universalist culture, rules are rules; they cannot and should not be bent and must be tolerated as they are. Everyone is treated equally based on universal prescriptions.

People are also divided based on the individualism vs. collectivism dichotomy. This is similar to Hofstede's dimensions, which address the effects of independence vs. interdependence in regard to a person's nature. Self-reliance is regarded as a positive trait for people who come from an individualistic culture. Contrastingly, people from a collectivistic culture believe that they need the support of others; thus, reliance on significant others, such as one's spouse, family members and close friends, is instrumental and necessary in numerous situations related to both work and life in general.

In addition, communication in the workplace is important; however, people differ in terms of how they relate to and interact with others. In a neutral culture, people do not necessarily need to express their feelings in a purely verbal form; rather, nonverbal cues can play an important role. For instance, people express themselves through hand gestures, facial expressions and bodily movements. Silence is another powerful way to express feelings without using speech. In contrast, in an affective culture, expressiveness is considered favourable as words can be verbalised or written to ensure that the meaning of the message or information is delivered in a way that can be comprehended completely.

Hall (1976) asserted that communication is contextual, as different approaches, mannerisms, and methods are used; thus, the boundaries between people and work that are set to enable effective communication to occur need to be clarified. In specific cultures, people set clear boundaries between professionalism and friendship in the workplace. In such cultures, people respect that when they are at work, the boss is the boss and work responsibilities need to be taken seriously. However, outside the work space, a boss and a subordinate might become close and establish a relationship without this affecting what transpires between them in the workplace. In other words, the two facets should be separated; they are not to be confused. However, in diffuse cultures, this might not be the case when it comes to the boundaries between work and play. In some cultures, people tend to have a less clear understanding of the rules regarding how issues related to friendship and superiority should be observed at work. As a result, the boundaries at times become blurred and interwoven. For example, in a diffuse culture, when an employee works with his father, the father may be unable to take action regarding his son's substandard work because of their relationship. Similarly, if a boss and employee are good friends, their judgment can become obscured due to the close relationship that they have established at work.

Finally, people can also relate to others based on achievement vs. ascription. The people in an achievement culture are promoted based on one criterion: what they can contribute to the organisation. In short, individuals are assessed based on their merits and qualifications. What counts most is the accomplishments that are demonstrated by the individuals – that is, how well they perform their tasks. Regarding the ascription culture, what matters is who the individuals know – for instance, the connections they have with other people and whom they trust within the organisation based on origin, gender, age, career and positions or titles. Thus, promotions are not necessarily earned through achievement; rather, they are based on the individuals' networks, and these connections can be a source of influence because of these individuals' professional experience. These employees are also accustomed to formal procedures, policies, regulations and customs. In essence, employees who are considered respected in the organisation can facilitate promotions.

With regard to environmental orientation, the following key question arises: How do people work to achieve promotions? From a cultural standpoint, people differ based on how they perceive and experience their environments. In an externally directed culture, we can explain the internal drive that individuals have when setting their goals. They decide on their aims and then set about to achieve them at whatever cost and regardless of the degree of risk taking that is required. People feel that they are in control of or are potentially able to control their environments because of their self-driven, self-motivated and self-reliant initiatives. Unlike people in an externally directed culture, those in an internally focused culture have a different view in regard to defining the ways in which goals should be met. Although they believe that they can work hard to achieve their goals, they also believe that this is often based on certain environmental conditions. They need to align goal achievement with other conditions, and one person cannot have total control over the outcomes of his or her goals. As such, fate, destiny and sometimes luck come into perspective. People can be destined to achieve certain targets at work or in their lives more generally, and they need to be in harmony with and attuned to the environment as well.

Time orientation is another cultural dilemma that needs to be considered. In a sequential culture, people tend to place a high priority on tasks and how they can be carried out in the most efficient and effective manner. Time is money. People align their agendas with their deadlines and develop procedures and systematic methods of achieving them. Conversely, in a synchronic culture, a different view of time can be observed. People in this culture are not in a hurry and oftentimes have a more relaxed attitude to punctuality and task accomplishment. What is prioritised is the establishment of a relationship between two parties. This process is inherently more crucial and takes time. Relationships need to be protected at all times; they should not be sacrificed. Extensions may be approved, and delays might take place and be accepted for the sake of relationships. Table 2.3 below extends our knowledge of the kinds of key questions that arise in the effort to understand cultural dimensions, cultural dilemmas, the challenges that result from working with people of different cultural orientations, and how to reconcile these differences in order to arrive at culturally effective solutions.

TABLE 2.1

Edward Hall (1976): Communicative-Cultural Dimensions

Key Reflective Questions	High Context (HC) Indirect, Implicit, Ambiguous, Subtle	Low Context (LC) Direct, Explicit, Detail, Succinct	How to Communicate Effectively?
Contextual-Orientation 1. What is the nature of information when you transmit messages to others? 2. What are the communication styles you use when speaking with others?	• Information is implicit in nature. • Information is delivered in a subtle manner because people are expected to have prior knowledge. • Communication is indirect, employs ambiguous language, and uses polite words when speaking to others. Believe in "relationship comes first; thus it should be protected."	• Information is explicitly and transparently delivered to others. • Information needs to be expressed in an open manner wherein extensive information is provided. • Communication style is direct, straightforward and blunt. Believe in "say what you feel" and "be honest to oneself."	**Rule #1**: Understand the importance of context dependent vs. content dependent: HC: Pay attention to *context*, identify the situations clearly before beginning your communication. For example, it is important to use polite words and subtle ways of addressing issues during conflicts. LC: Make sure you value *content*, put emphasis on the text and prepare detailed speech where all content is explicitly described or verbalised during communication. Provide clear instructions for both written and verbal statements.

(Continued)

TABLE 2.1 *(Continued)*

Edward Hall (1976): Communicative-Cultural Dimensions

Key Reflective Questions	High Context (HC) Indirect, Implicit, Ambiguous, Subtle	Low Context (LC) Direct, Explicit, Detail, Succinct	How to Communicate Effectively?
3. What is your cultural orientation when engaging with others?	• People prefer to build relationship before they can develop trust with others. Relationships need to be protected and maintained at all times.	• Focus on accomplishing goals and objectives. Thus, relationship is secondary for trust formation, put priority on task engagement before relationship can be developed.	**Rule #2:** Pay attention to the way people view relationship vs. task orientation. HC: Apply *face-saving* strategy to protect and maintain relationships. • Avoid confrontation as much as possible to guard the close-ties relationship with people. • Be vigilant in the way you express concerns and feelings during conflicts, use an intermediary to speak with people who have issues to avoid embarrassment. LC: People will go all the way to express their opinions, thoughts, feelings and actions since explicit and open communication is appreciated. • Engage in direct confrontation as it is important to immediately address any concerns to accomplish objectives. • Use tactics that enable people to work on the commitments and task assigned where background information is made explicit in interaction.

(Continued)

TABLE 2.1 (Continued)

Edward Hall (1976): Communicative-Cultural Dimensions

Key Reflective Questions	High Context Polychronic (P-Time)	Low Context Monochronic (M-Time)	How to Manage Time?
Time Consciousness 1. Do you perceive time as linear or cyclical? 2. Do you adhere to a strict agenda with datelines or prefer flexibility and a situational-based timeline? 3. Do you appreciate punctuality and being on time or tolerate extended timelines and procrastination?	• Time is elastic – it operates in multiple dimensions and at times in a chaotic fashion. • Tasks are engaged in simultaneously; that is, "do many things at a time" – become a multitasker. • Time has no specific order; it runs from one end to another and priority is determined by a person or circumstances.	• Time is rigid – it operates in a sequential and linear manner, often pursued in a systematic way. • Tasks are pursued in an orderly fashion, engaged in a "one thing at a time" manner. • Time is divided into intervals, and each has a separate activity which needs to be followed accordingly.	**Rule #1 for people ascribed to M-time:** • Should learn to tolerate *time insensitivity* and lack of punctuality. • Should develop a flexible plan which gives ample room for any glitches in the agenda set; that is, prepare contingency plans. • Should try to line up activities that could be conducted in a realistic and feasible manner (when things are conducted in a nonsystematic way). • Should inculcate a high level of patience under certain circumstances where time often lags behind, that is, meetings, deliverables, queues, traffic, etc. **Rule #1 for people ascribed to P-time:** • Should learn to respect and appreciate *time diligence* and punctuality. • Should develop an extensive agenda and formulate key activities, wherein datelines must be carefully observed. • Should learn that time is a measurable substance; thus, it could be wasted, spent, saved and made up, but according to the plans made. *(Continued)*

TABLE 2.1 *(Continued)*

Edward Hall (1976): Communicative-Cultural Dimensions

Key Reflective Questions	High Privacy (HP)	Low Privacy (LP)	How to Manage Work Boundaries?
Spatial-Orientation 1. How do you develop a clear distinction between private and public domains? 2. How do you determine spatial boundaries between work and life?	• Embrace a strong sense of private and personal space, set clear rules for who can enter both spaces. • Spatial order is important and cannot be negotiated, assign location and place according to its importance. • Sharing a space is less acceptable. Distinction needs to be clearly segmented.	• Accommodate and accept less ruling on personal space, but have a tighter rule who can enter their private space. • Spatial order can be modified according to needs and purposes, flexible about the conditions and rules surrounding the event or person affected. • Sharing a space is highly encouraged, if not warranted.	**Rule #1:** General rule: Understand the value of privacy and disclosure. Make sure to observe the factors that allow people to disclose what is important or why they retain or control information that is private. **Rule #2: Specific rule:** **High Privacy:** • Understand that people value privacy and guard their boundaries tightly, and people need to respect the conditions. • People also expect that boundaries will be managed carefully, and work and life are separate entities that need different forms of spatial orientation and boundary management. • Keep personal space private; touching is less practiced among people belonging to a "distant culture" who value high privacy. *(Continued)*

TABLE 2.1 (*Continued*)

Edward Hall (1976): Communicative-Cultural Dimensions

Key Reflective Questions	High Privacy (HP)	Low Privacy (LP)	How to Manage Work Boundaries?
3. What are the challenges in delineating private vs. public space?	• For example, rooms are assigned in the office based on a single person, doors are kept closed, a person needs to be invited instead of impromptu or walk-in visitation. • People respect quiet moments, and distant-proximity needs to be observed carefully; that is, build widespread space.	• For example, officemates may be placed in a big shared space at work. Visitors can casually knock on the door or announce their presence unexpectedly. • People can live within a space that is crowded and noisy without fuss, and close proximity can be tolerated.	**Low Privacy:** • Understand privacy is shared and release it only to people with whom they have strong ties like family members, spouses, close friends and not strangers. • Understand that people disclose information based on instrumental values and information can be easily exchanged and shared. • People practice "warm cultures", and touching is acceptable among people; close proximity is welcomed and encouraged.

Source: Zakaria, N. 2000. *International Journal of Manpower*, 21(6), 492–510; Zakaria, N., Stanton, J. & Sarkar-Barney, S.T.M. 2003. *Information, Technology & People*, 16(1), pp. 49–75; Hooker, J. 2003. *Working Across Cultures*, Stanford, CA: Stanford Press Publisher.

TABLE 2.2

Hofstede (1984): Six Cultural Dimensions

Cultural Dimensions	Key Reflective Questions	How to Resolve Cultural Differences?
1. Power Distance (PD)	• Do you accept disparity where power and status are promoted unequally and respect for the superior roles is highly addressed? • Do you expect the practice of empowerment is implemented at work whereby people are treated equitably and participate equally in management? • Do you employ a hierarchical organizational structure and observe power is distributed from top to bottom? • Do you introduce a flat-based structure with an egalitarian style of management and observe decentralized decision-making responsibility?	**Rule #1:** **High PD:** Learn to accept the hierarchical structure where it defines the way things operate and instructions are channelled down, that is, from top to bottom and decisions based on consensus. There is a high acceptance of privileges attached to power and position given. **Rule #2:** **Low PD:** Learn to appreciate that empowerment is exercised and people are treated equally, with the ability to voice their opinions much more freely and become independent decision-makers. Individuals are highly conscious of their individual rights.

(Continued)

TABLE 2.2 (Continued)

Hofstede (1984): Six Cultural Dimensions

Cultural Dimensions	Key Reflective Questions	How to Resolve Cultural Differences?
2. Individualist vs. Collectivist (I-C)	• How important is for you to refer to and consult with others and work collectively when making decisions? Do you need to reach a consensus prior to making final decisions? • How important is it for you to have the freedom to make decisions independently? Do you expect autonomy when considering choices and alternatives before arriving at a decision? • How important is group cohesion, harmony, relationships, and loyalty when you work with others? How does it affect your working style? • Do you expect people to employ honesty and tell the truth when confronted with a conflict so that decisions can be independently and fairly assessed?	**Rule #1:** Understand the need for interdependence vs. independence when making decisions at work. **Individualistic:** People will often need a space and autonomy to think, deliberate and then make a decision since they are used to an autonomous style of decision-making. **Collectivistic:** People will need to refer to the superior and work in group discussion before any final decision can be arrived. A process of arriving at a consensus is typical, and most of the time, the top management makes the final call. **Rule #2:** Believe in certain traits and values –honesty vs. harmony and truth vs. loyalty – when communicating information so that decisions can be made using effective strategy. **Individualistic:** Believe in telling the truth and be honest when faced with situations so that an independent judgment can be evaluated on the basis of self, I and me. **Collectivistic:** Believe in harmony and relationships and decisions needing to be reached with others especially at higher ranks or positions. Believe in others, we and us.

(Continued)

TABLE 2.2 (Continued)

Hofstede (1984): Six Cultural Dimensions

Cultural Dimensions	Key Reflective Questions	How to Resolve Cultural Differences?
3. Uncertainty Avoidance (UA)	• Do you value stability and certainty when dealing with unknown situations at work? • Do you require rules, prescribed orders and instructions from your superior when working on tasks? • Do you prefer challenges, creativity and innovative mindsets when embarking on daily work and projects? • Do you employ an informal attitude towards volatility, and can you accept changes and risk more casually and easily?	**Rule #1:** **High UA:** Understand the fear of uncertainty, high level of insecurities, and lack of acceptance for ambiguity when faced with new uncertain contexts and new circumstances. Promote stability and predictability in plans and produce a defined structure to guide people on what to do and how to do it to reduce anxieties. **Rule #2:** **Low UA:** Adopt risk-taking attitudes as people have positive perceptions of challenges when introducing and expecting changes to take place at work. Promote innovation, as "thinking out of the box" strategy is for people who value challenges and have high risk tolerance.
4. Masculinity vs. Femininity (Mas-Fem)	• Do you put priority on high performance and success and wealth achievements when pursuing your career? • Do you appreciate caring, affection and relationship building when engaging with people at work? • Are you expected to be tough and employ an assertive and aggressive manner when dealing with subordinates and colleagues? • Are you expected to be tactful, sensitive, kind and modest and show a cooperative way of collaboration?	**Rule #1:** Understand the roles played by masculinity and femininity in terms of goal-oriented vs. relationship-oriented outlooks, that is, material achievements for quantity life vs. nurturing and modest character for quality life. **MAS society:** Gender roles are distinctly evident between male vs. females. People attribute pride, reputation and egos based on their status and position. **FEM society:** Gender roles are overlapping and not evidently distinctive. Success is not definitive or set in stone, but can be negotiated with others. **Rule #2:** Understand how societal rules on traditions like age, gender and roles inform work expectations vs. how innovation and creativity are expected to be demonstrated by individuals.

(Continued)

TABLE 2.2 (*Continued*)

Hofstede (1984): Six Cultural Dimensions

Cultural Dimensions	Key Reflective Questions	How to Resolve Cultural Differences?
5. Short term vs. Long term (ST-LT)	• What is the basic level of inclination of a society in pursuing goodness? Do you choose between values and rights, and virtues and obligations? • How do you view your time horizon when dealing with business partners between the principles consistency, truth and pragmatism, modesty, and thriftiness? • What is the main focus for business agenda? Are you able to understand the importance of future prospects vs. past and present agendas? • What is the importance between long-term growth and perseverance vs. quick results and short-term success?	**Rule #1:** Believe in quantity of life or quality of life. **ST:** Appreciate instrumental values and immediate result and have personal stability. **LT:** Emphasize on relationship building, aim at developing meaningful future collaboration, and favour group expectations (instead of personal). **Rule #2:** Respect for tradition and quick end results vs. believing in persistence and commitment for a long time duration. **ST:** Focus on past and present-oriented timeframe and have a static, and conventional mentality. Mutual gift-giving, favours, and greetings is expected. **LT:** Focus on futuristics and long-term plans, dynamic and pragmatic mentality, support networking. Emphasis on perseverance and persistence on business deals and diligence in financial planning; that is, a "prudence and thrift" attitude is encouraged.

(*Continued*)

TABLE 2.2 (*Continued*)

Hofstede (1984): Six Cultural Dimensions

Cultural Dimensions	Key Reflective Questions	How to Resolve Cultural Differences?
6. Indulgence vs. Restraint	• What are the magnitude and tendency for a society to fulfil their desires? • Do you freely express the feeling of gratification? Do you perceive enjoyment and having fun during work and life as important? • Do you suppress the feeling of gratification? Why is it important for you to control and be calculative about time spent between work and life? • Do you control certain elements to fulfil your desires or do you exhaust all possibilities that you feel deserving after a hard day of work?	**Rule #1:** Understand the rules society places on expressing gratification – truly expressing it without limitations and enjoying life as it is offered vs. withholding desires accordingly and needing to regulate through stringent social norms and be less candid about it. **Rule #2:** Understand the level of impulse reactions and extent of pursuance of desires – people who like to be free when making decisions about what and how things matter to them vs. people who take calculative steps and measures to how desires need to be kept in check.

Source: Minkov, M. and Hofstede, G. 2011. *Cross-cultural Management: An International Journal*, 18(1), 10–20.

TABLE 2.3

Trompenaars and Hampden-Turner's (1997) Cultural Dimensions: Using the PET Framework

	Key Reflective Questions	Dilemmas Faced in Cultural Situations	How to Reconcile Cultural Differences
People Orientation			
1. Universalist vs. Particularist	• Do you abide by rules or do you make decisions dependent on circumstances, i.e. case by case? • Do you apply standards and values equally to everyone, or do you scrutinise cases based on personal relationships and obligations?	• Should people acknowledge that the role of a rule is more important than the role of connections and networks? • Should people acknowledge that procedures will be adhered to and cannot be changed or should rules be bent, wherein flexibility is expected?	**Rule #1:** Take into consideration what matters more – standards and task orientation or circumstances and relationship orientation. **Rule #2:** Take into consideration whether people should comply with rules, commonly known as "by the book" or whether situations should be evaluated on a case-by-case basis.
2. Individualist vs. Collectivist	• Do you work independently or collectively? • Do you look out for yourself more than for others, or do you put the well-being of others, such as your spouse, family and close friends, before your own?	• Should people believe that the self is important, or is being a team player more desirable? • Should people believe that an individual has the right to make decisions for him- or herself, or should significant others have the right to participate in important decisions related to an individual's work and life?	**Rule #1:** Believe in the importance of empowerment and self-reliance vs. delegation and group reliance when making important decisions. **Rule #2:** Believe in the way in which people take care of themselves – putting the self over others and working independently or prioritising others over the self and working interdependently.

(Continued)

TABLE 2.3 *(Continued)*

Trompenaars and Hampden-Turner's (1997) Cultural Dimensions: Using the PET Framework

	Key Reflective Questions	Dilemmas Faced in Cultural Situations	How to Reconcile Cultural Differences
3. Affective vs. Neutral	• Do you express your feelings spontaneously and publicly, or do you prefer to bottle up your feelings, yet opening up only to selective people? • Do you minimalise the exchange of messages?	• Should people express emotions freely and openly, or should they engage in polite speech to protect relationships? • Should people speak directly using verbal or written cues, or should they communicate indirectly via subtle messages such as nonverbal cues?	**Rule #1:** Explore whether communication is predicated on detailed content or whether it is dependent on context and circumstances. **Rule #2:** Explore whether people can express their feelings freely or whether they should remain silent.
4. Specific vs. Diffuse	• Do you share your thoughts and emotions selectively with different groups, or do you make no distinction between the public and private spheres? • How do you communicate with others across formal and informal boundaries?	• Should people develop clear guidelines by communicating informally and casually, or should communication be formal and personalised? • Should people develop trust and respect based on boundaries that are public, or should these be private?	**Rule #1:** Be alert regarding boundaries at work – play and work should be separated and divided equally for the best performance, or play and work should be interweaved and thus would impact decision-making. **Rule #2:** Be aware that people set boundaries regarding disclosure – the public and private spheres are either discernible or intertwined.

(Continued)

TABLE 2.3 (*Continued*)

Trompenaars and Hampden-Turner's (1997) Cultural Dimensions: Using the PET Framework

	Key Reflective Questions	Dilemmas Faced in Cultural Situations	How to Reconcile Cultural Differences
5. Achievement vs. Ascription	• Do you rely on merit, or do you rely on personal networks? • Do you believe in objective outcomes and deliverables, or do you believe in subjectivity and affiliated status?	• Should people be evaluated based on what they have accomplished, or should evaluation be based on whom they are affiliated with? • Should people be evaluated based on their productivity, or should evaluation be based on unmeasurable achievements, position and status?	**Rule #1:** Be aware of how achievements are evaluated – objectively vs. subjectively. **Rule #2:** Be aware of the criteria for promotion – contributions and performance vs. status quo and connections.
Environmental Orientation			
6. Outer vs. Inner	• How do you control environments? • Do you believe that problems are caused by external sources or by internal ones? • Do you control your environment, or are you controlled by it? • Do you control nature, or do you let it take its own course?	• Should people believe in hard work and achievements, or should they rely on fate, luck and harmony with the environment? • Should people embrace challenges and seek empowerment as they are willing to be held accountable on a task undertaken or should people be led by a superior's direction as they feel more comfortable engaging in predictable task? • Should people choose to achieve goals based on self-driven initiatives, or should they rely on consensus and team effort?	**Rule #1:** Understand the drive for people to achieve their goals – internal or external drive. **Rule #2:** Understand people's perceptions of risk and empowerment at work vs. being guided and directed to meet the task given. **Rule #3:** Understand whether people are independent or interdependent in regard to accomplishing their goals.

(Continued)

TABLE 2.3 (Continued)

Trompenaars and Hampden-Turner's (1997) Cultural Dimensions: Using the PET Framework

	Key Reflective Questions	Dilemmas Faced in Cultural Situations	How to Reconcile Cultural Differences
7. Sequential vs. Synchronic	• What is the nature of time? • How do you perceive and manage time in the workplace? • Do you complete tasks in order and systematically, or do you do so simultaneously and without order?	• Should people rely on sequential processes or should they rely on synchronic processes when negotiating? • Should people focus on single tasks and follow orders, or should they be engaged in jobs that require the individual to focus on multiple areas by multitasking jobs? • Should people prioritise precision and time management, or should they focus on loosely determined and less urgent time-bound tasks?	**Rule #1:** Clearly define the way in which time is managed – in an orderly and systematic manner vs. in a cyclical and contextual way. **Rule #2:** Clearly inform about the way in which tasks should be managed – one at a time vs. simultaneously. **Rule #3:** Clearly educate people on the meaning of urgency and deadlines vs. a relaxed, "as it goes" and "take it easy" attitude.

Source: Zakaria, N. 2017. *Culture Matters? Decision Making in Global Virtual Teams: Managing the Challenges and Synergies during Globally Distributed Collaboration.* Boca Raton, FL: CRC Press, Taylor & Francis Group.

BLOG VIGNETTE 2.2   Global Village Dubai: Finally, Here I Am!

I was finally able to visit the often-talked-about Global Village, a large, outdoor cultural shopping centre and theme park in Dubai that is purported to be one of the largest tourist, entertainment, and leisure projects in the world. A taxi driver gave my husband and me an impressive review of the park when we first visited Dubai in January 2009. He told us that the park was divided into continents and countries and sold countless products from every corner of the globe. Each section, he told us, offered an abundant food menu that catered to a wide variety of taste buds. Unfortunately, my husband and I were pressed for time and were, therefore, unable to visit the park during that trip. However, we kept the venue on our wish list, intending to visit when we returned.

In October 2009, my husband and I were finally living in Dubai. The Dubai Shopping Festival, which offered an abundance of spectacular deals, was wrapping up for the summer, and I begged my husband to visit the park with me for one sole and "soul" reason: "I am a culture person!" It was a must that I visit this melting pot during one of its busiest times of the year. Therefore, we went, and after three hours of gallivanting around every continent, I came to the following conclusion: there was little distinction between the offerings from all over the world, from Malaysia to Syria. Each country's section featured a booth selling clothes and toys from China or perfumes that could be found anywhere. To my horror, I found nothing authentic in the Singapore and Malaysia booths and had no feeling that the latter was my homeland; rather, it felt as if it were a strange land.

It is amazing how the globe is changing as customers' tastes and preferences converge. What I experienced at Global Village appeared to reflect the true effect of globalisation – geographical distances and borders around the globe are minimised or even eliminated. If you miss an opportunity to purchase an item in Thailand, you can certainly purchase it in Egypt; similarly, if you miss the opportunity to purchase an item in the Thailand store in Global Village, you are almost guaranteed to find it in the Egypt store. Markets in Dubai are no longer customising products for local customers; rather, they are catering to global customers. Dubai embraces the melting-pot concept and the "global products for global customers" rule.

In reality, I also realised, based on my extensive travel experience, that there are two contradictory ways of viewing the world. On the one hand, I view it as a global landscape with minimal distinctions among the various countries, as behaviours seem to be homogenous and uniform. On the other hand, I see the world as unique and distinctive due to its diverse cultural influences, and behaviours are heterogeneous and diversified in terms of human values, beliefs and customs. Let me put this into a different context, based on the recent description provided by my colleague, Dr. Sabiha Mumtaz, when she reviewed Global Village. A regular patron of Global Village, she was intrigued by the cultural experiences that she had each time she visited the park in the autumn. She witnessed the evolution of the cultural architecture, designs and attractions that were incorporated into the representative pavilions, each of which differed completely from what I had witnessed almost a decade before. Years ago, as far as I could recall, Global Village was not developed to the extent that it was now.

As she entered the Global Village, my colleague was mesmerised by the vast cultural experiences from over 27 countries, each offering representations of its cultural heritage and replicas, such as the Taj Mahal in Agra, Big Ben in London, the Eiffel Tower in Paris, the Petronas Towers in Kuala Lumpur, the Coliseum in Rome and numerous other iconic country markers and artefacts. She truly enjoyed discovering the array of local and international foods and cultural events, which allowed her to purchase different souvenirs, sample a variety of foods and drinks (including tea and coffee), enjoy various cultural dances, cherish the theatre acts and the performances of acrobats, and so on. She ended the conversation with me enthusiastically: "It is as if you are watching the world that lies ahead of you, indeed, it is as if you are entering the world, rather than walking in the Arabic world of Dubai!" At the end, I could conclude that this was indeed our pleasant experiences; Global Village promoted a multicuisine, multicultural and multiethnic environment which offers a global shopping experience in one place.

CULTURAL LESSON 2.3: IS CULTURE DIVERGING OR CONVERGING?

I read once in the local newspaper of United Arab Emirates, *Khaleej Times,* that Dubai's population is composed of over 200 nationalities. Imagine that! What a truly Global Village, as envisioned by Ohmae Kenichi years ago. Moreover, with the advancement of information technology, the world becomes borderless, allowing different nationalities to come together and communicate easily via the Internet. If such diversity is the case, how do you fit yourself in this melting-pot country? This thought brings me back to the topic of cultural diversity when we were discussing the issue of cultural impacts on management styles, where a few essential issues emerged:

- Do we have cultural distinction in Dubai, where everyone is different and yet working hand in hand?
- Do we really have cultural values to follow and comply with?
- Aren't we all converging now, and hence what matters is how to work together given such differences?

It is appalling to realize that people are now becoming similar in many respects because they live in environments where everyone brings different values, and thus to work harmoniously, they must be more adaptable and accepting. Is that really true? Several of my students mentioned that they no longer recognize their original roots or genuine/authentic cultural values since they had lived in Dubai for many years. Their lives had changed and different moulds had shaped them differently – for better or for worse. It was difficult for them to illustrate or describe what their cultural values are now. Their multicultured confrontations and encounters with people of diverse backgrounds seemed to present both advantages and disadvantages.

Thus, my question to you is: If we no longer can recognize our root culture, does that mean we are more tolerant and accepting of other cultures? Can our multicultural society mould us into a truly new culture? In that respect, can one's root multicultural values continue to influence his or her management style? I wonder and ponder because I truly can no longer find my Malaysian working values within myself. My behaviour adapts to the situation I am in.

If I find myself in a high power distance culture, for example, I accept and respect the red tape and bureaucracy. Believe me, this does not mean I am without frustrations or that I have become a more patient human being. On the other side of the spectrum, if and when I am working in a low power distance environment, like I do now at my university, I follow that style perfectly as well. So, is this evidence that when we work in a multicultural society, we are able to mould ourselves as needed? Have I become what we call a culturally competent expatriate or manager?

I am seeking more perspectives on the idea of either *becoming a true cultural melting pot society* – the phenomenon of people from multiple cultures melting together and blending into one uniform culture or *becoming a salad bowl society* – where people from multiple cultures can affect each other (which improves society overall) while still maintaining their individuality. My honest and humble observation is: the world is indeed becoming a melting pot rather than a salad bowl! But uniquely in Dubai, I observe that expatriates are representing the "salad bowl society" wherein they endure their exclusive cultures. A truly cosmopolitan city, with its vibrance, it is full of the hustle-bustle of life so that every person, every nation and every culture lives harmoniously and tolerates and embraces cultural diversity with bliss and enjoyment. In essence, I do feel it that way – when I first arrived in the land of Dubai up until now.

CULTURAL REFLECTION 2.1: CULTURE, LET'S DEFINE IT!

When you think of culture, what comes to your mind?

- Can you define what culture is? Specifically, what do you mean by culture?
- What is an example of culture? Please provide a few examples that illustrate your authentic culture, that is, food, clothing, festival events and many others.
- What does culture include and/or exclude? What is exclusive in your own culture?
  - Can you describe some unique customary practices and heritage traditions that are reflective of your culture? For example, marriage ceremony, greetings, meeting procedures, and so on.
- What are your cultural values? Please provide which values are meaningful to you and which are less impactful to you.
- How about the cultural values that you observe from others that are different from you? Can you share a story that illustrates such differences?

CULTURAL REFLECTION 2.2: UNDERSTANDING CULTURAL INFLUENCE AT WORKPLACE

As an expatriate, reflect on one specific situation that you have faced or heard about in the workplace where cultural blunders were made by you or your colleagues. For example, someone came to a meeting late, which upsets the "punctual" boss.

- What would you do if it were you?
- Discuss why such blunders result in negative outcomes.
- Based on your culture, what do you do when you encounter an uncomfortable situation, as illustrated above? How do you express yourself?
- What action should be taken to rectify the mistakes made? In understanding about workplace blunders, can you think about organizational culture?
- What does organizational culture mean to you?
- Do you think an organizational culture is important? If yes, how does it influence your behaviour, and if no, why not?
- How does organizational culture affect your practices in the workplace? For example, provide a scenario or circumstances at workplace that you realized was affected by culture.

2.1 @CULTURAL PONDERS

We Are Equals, Aren't We?

Robert Thompson
Autumn 2010

The issue of power distance and its relationship with a cultural dimension called 'diffuse vs. specific'is the most difficult aspect of work culture for me to understand and deal with. In my culture, power distance is minimised as much as possible. Managers will make huge efforts to make their staff feel equal, part of the process and not subordinates. Managers will introduce their employees as colleagues; they will ask for their advice. For example, in my old job, the managing director chose not to have an office, but rather to sit at a work station with the rest of the staff. There are many examples of this, but essentially, effort is made for low power distance as employees in my culture will strive harder and work more efficiently when given this type of environment. A lot of workplaces won't ask any questions if an employee turns up late one day, because there is low distance and the trust that this person will work back late another day. This is a generalisation, of course, but it is on the most part and where most companies are heading. Working in Dubai is a very different experience. I am a middle-level manager so I have bosses but also people who work for me. When dealing with my bosses, I expected to be treated with low power distance but was not. At first, it was really difficult to handle. I felt like I was not trusted, or that my boss did not believe in my abilities. I just did not understand it. When dealing with my staff – I didn't want them to feel the same way so made extra effort to have a low power distance. It worked the opposite way. My efforts to make them feel comfortable and happy worked in reverse. It was difficult as I realized that 'what made us feel comfortable was very different.' In retrospective, to me, one of the most challenging aspect is to change my perception, adjust my tolerance level, and rectify my actions to become culturally-aligned with the people I am managing and working with.

3

Who Is a Self-Initiated Expatriate?

Regardless of the pleasurable and strenuous expatriation journey, your cultural experience will definitely result in knowing yourself through the lens of other's culture.

Norhayati Zakaria

BLOG VIGNETTE 3.1   Relocation: The Reality and the Dream

A few years back, when I was living in Malaysia, a colleague, Rhea Kanosuki, moved from Japan approached me and announced the following: "After doing my homework, I finally chose to work in your country because I thought it would be a good fit for me. After all, I like the all-year-round warm weather, and I was happy to hear about the wonderful truly Asian-fusion cuisines, that is, Malay, Chinese and Indian, described by my friends who had lived and migrated there for years. I was ready and excited to relocate, only then to realize that, after few days of elation, culture shock began to slip in and that the move had been a long and arduous journey! Many things bothered me about Malaysia, that is, the lack of punctuality, the bureaucracy, the way people solve problems and the manner people communicate – they were just so different from me." With that voice still ringing in my ear, I began to reminisce about medieval times, when our ancestors migrated to foreign countries for greener pastures. Like my friend, these migrants still needed to learn to adjust and live in an estranged land. In fact, my grandfather migrated from Sumatera to Malaya, where the generations that followed stayed for decades. Similarly, I recall the time in the early 1980s, when my schoolmate Leow Mui Lin announced with a sparkle in her eyes, "Hey, I am moving abroad for three years. My father was assigned to work in Hong Kong!" Back then, this seemed like a far-fetched thought, at least for me. Some perplexing questions seemed to tirelessly plead for answers over the growing years:

- What is so good living in a foreign land?
- Why would one move out of one's own comfort zone?
- Where would be an ideal place to relocate, reside and/or migrate?
- How do you make sense of the new life, the new workplace, the new people?

Hmmm, back then, I had never been overseas, yet dreamed about it relentlessly and failed to make sense of any of the mystifying questions. Now, after decades of relocation and years of across-the-board travelling, I have come to my true senses of what it is like to become an expatriate. In a nutshell, it is a transformation of my inexorable dreams into a reality, indeed, a beautiful one!

CULTURAL LESSON 3.1: WHO ARE SELF-INITIATED EXPATRIATES?

The emergence of self-initiated expatriates further intensifies the challenges faced by multinational organizations because people are searching for better career prospects and are willing to relocate in order to obtain competitive salary or compensation packages. With the emergence of SIEs, multinational corporations need to acknowledge the influence of culture on management practices because expatriates will bring their own cultural baggage and uniqueness to the company's doorstep. By integrating both fields abovementioned, this book is expected to provide a valuable understanding in order to educate SIEs on the richness of cultural behaviours and also the challenges confronted and synergies obtained culturally at a global workplace. Culture has a paramount impact on how leaders manage their colleagues and teams in the workplace. One's attitudes, values, beliefs and perceptions all matter when people work with culturally diverse backgrounds colleagues. Cultural differences cannot be ignored, as a work structure that thrives only in a monoculture environment hardly exists for the multinational corporations of today. Instead, the multicultural environment takes priority, with a soaring demand for global talents and workforces that need to be recruited.

It has been clearly established in the field of international human resources that there are increasing trends and phenomena of burgeoning SIEs in newly occupied cosmopolitan cities in the world such as Dubai, Qatar, Jeddah, Singapore, Hong Kong, Shanghai, Tokyo and many others. Hence, this topic is timely to be published because it allows the combined fields of international human resource management and cross-cultural management to offer new perspectives on strategies, challenges and advantages of cultural journey of SIEs in light of crucial management practices such as decision-making, negotiation, leadership, global teams, intercultural communication and expatriation. In the context of expatriating for a multinational organization, generally, a worker wouldn't grab such an opportunity for the sake of obtaining international exposure. Instead, the perplexing question is: *Don't most people want to stay where they are and not relocate?* In contrast, for some people, such an assignment is accepted as a symbol of pride and honour, though it comes with a baggage of sacrifice. It is like stamping a "global ticket" on your passport, signifying the credibility of your international career. Yet, organizational expatriation is also seen as a risky game that involves plunging into the uncertainties of a new work environment and often an entirely new life.

We have seen over the past few decades, however, that expatriation no longer requires receiving an assignment from your existing company. Instead, due to a viable – albeit competitive – international job market and the rise of global talent management, people can initiate their own expatriation processes, that is, make the decision to secure new jobs in a new country or location, quit their current jobs, and relocate for better careers, salaries or lives. Executives or managers no longer need to wait to be selected by their boss for a foreign assignment. Considering this, how do we recognize global talent in terms of self-initiated expatriates, and how are they different compared to organizational expatriates (OEs)? Further, how and why do these two categories matter in the context of cultural adjustment? More than a decade ago, Richardson (2004) defined an SIE simply as "someone who elects to go overseas independently" (p. 469). To elaborate further, Andresen et al. (2014) described an SIE as an individual who takes a job in a foreign country, choosing to do so based on his or her own willingness, and who is usually not sponsored by any organization. In essence, this self-selected job behaviour is a voluntary act undertaken in order to find a better job in a host country, although it may not necessarily always be about the job. Some SIEs make such bold decisions of "expatriating" for other reasons, that is, lifestyle, weather, food and many others. In essence, SIEs can be considered a means for career advancement which takes one away from his or her own home country.

Key drawbacks related to both forms of expatriation include adjusting to unfamiliar geographical locations, living surroundings, and rules and conditions in the workplace, as well as living far from family and friends. While in this sense, the process of expatriation remains the same for both OEs and SIEs, their motivation to move often differs. While OEs are requested to leave by their top management, SIEs tend to make independent decisions to seek outward opportunities. Rather, they can choose what positions to apply for and where they prefer to be relocated, and they can choose when to repatriate, that is, return to their home country. SIEs also face the risks associated with quitting their job in their home country, meaning they may or may not have a job if they choose to return. OEs, on the other hand, can stay with their same companies and thus are generally guaranteed a job when they return. Such security is not available to SIEs (most of the time), unless their former employer welcomes them back to work again in the same firm.

Hence, a key question is: What do SIEs need to understand about the process of adjustment when they relocate, even though they "self-select" themselves to leave their home country? For example, in a culture where people are risk averse and avoid ambiguous situations, they may take time to decide whether they will need to make sacrifices as compared to people who prefers challenges and don't mind taking risks when relocating. Hence, one's cultural background will play a greater role. Nonetheless, not only will one's cultural values and background affect the decision of moving abroad as an SIE, but the newly culturally oriented environment they choose to enter will also be a perplexing experience. People need to fully familiarize and adjust themselves by cultivating high cognitive, emotional and behaviour competencies.

BLOG VIGNETTE 3.2   Experiencing the Honeymoon Stage!

I remembered another incident with Rhea Kanosuki, a Japanese colleague who worked with me in Malaysia. On only her second day in my home country, she came rushing towards me in the cafeteria and revealed that she had had such a pleasant time in class.

"Why are you so happy, Rhea?" I asked.
"How could I not be happy?" she responded. "Your culture and my culture are the same! Our students are obedient, polite, and pleasant. They gave me full attention and showed high interest in class, enough to keep me motivated for the one and half hours of lecturing."

I observed her for the next few days, and she remained collected and joyful. For the first week, it seemed that she didn't mind the different working styles in Malaysia, for example not being punctual when attending meetings. After several weeks, though, things begin to irritate her. With a solemn face, she showed up at my room one evening.

"Hey, you don't look too good, Rhea," I said, wondering what was wrong with her. "May I know what's the matter?"
Her response was slow, but eventually, she blurted it out. "I was bothered that some of my students missed deadlines and didn't show a serious attitude on assignments. My students were not able to respond to me when I asked about the deadlines. You know, Yati, we Japanese are very critical over deadlines and punctuality. Here the administration is not punctual, and then I saw the same attitude with some of my students!"

CULTURAL LESSON 3.2: RIDING THE U-CURVE

As Rhea's story suggests, the adjustment and acculturation process is made up of different stages. Lysgaard (1955) introduced the *u-curve model of cultural adjustment* (refer to Figure 3.1), in which an expatriate experiences and undergoes four distinct phases of cultural adjustment: the honeymoon, culture shock, recovery and mastery.

To be a successful expatriate, it is crucial to know the stages you will experience so that you can cope with them as you move through. An international human resources manager needs to not only understand the different stages, but also know what actions can be taken to remedy the cultural shocks experienced at each stage. The first phase is known as the "honeymoon," a *euphoric* stage that is the most exciting for anyone who has a positive outlook about the expatriation process.

At this stage, the host organization needs to welcome such enthusiasm shown by the SIE. On the other hand, someone who is anxious about the whole idea of relocating may not experience the honeymoon stage; instead, they may immediately experience a stage of irritation and hostility, in which they may remain for a period of time. In retrospect, when I first reached Dubai, my honeymoon stage lasted only two to three weeks, which is quite short. For only a brief time span, I felt like I was on air; everything was good and rosy. Of course, no honeymoon lasts forever. The second stage is called "culture shock," wherein expatriates begin to experience hostility and uneasiness due to discrepancies between what they expect and what they observe or experience in the workplace. This stage is thus most critical to be managed by the organizations as well as the managers who are dealing with expatriates. They need to be observant to be able to notice any abnormalities in behaviours – to identify whether one's emotions are disturbed and impact work performance.

The interesting thing about the process of culture shock is that sometimes you may not even realize you are experiencing it. People are more comfortable saying, "Oh, I'm just going through a difficult period," not understanding that it is the cultural aspects of the transition that are causing so much pain. People often assume that expatriation is only about adjusting to the new place and the new job. But what is it about the new place or new job that seems so daunting? Could cultural aspects be at play? For example, adjusting to a new work environment means figuring out the

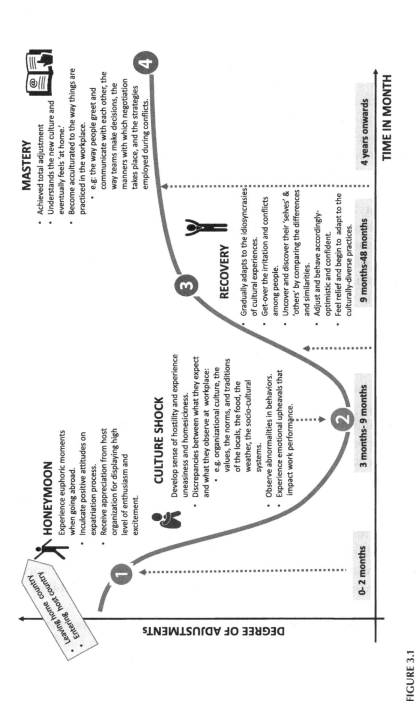

FIGURE 3.1

Experiencing cross-cultural expeditions for SIEs using U-curve cultural adjustment model. (Adapted from Lysgaard, S. 1955. *International Social Science Bulletin, 7*, 45–51.)

organizational culture – understanding "how we do things here," that is, the rules and customs of the workplace. There is also the outer layer out of this new workplace: the country, the values, the norms and the traditions of the locals, which you can only grasp by understanding the behaviour of the people around you. Apart from this, you also need to accustom yourself to the most basic functions of life in the new country: the food, the weather, the social systems and so on. For me, the second stage set in when the semester began and I started to teach. Guess what the source of my confusion and frustration was? The system, my colleagues and my students. They had different ways of communicating, different structures of authority, different decision-making styles and completely different negotiation styles. I also experienced weather shock. I did not realize it at the time, but the weather made me feel more tired than usual, which affected my work.

The third stage is called "recovery," where an expatriate gradually adapts to the idiosyncrasies experienced during the uneasy period of culture shock. At this point, expatriates begin to see the positive side of the irritation they coped with. This is a crucial learning process for them because they uncover and discover their "selves" and "others" by comparing the differences and similarities. Consequently, they learn how to adjust and behave accordingly. At this stage, expatriates feel relief because they have been able to endure the pain they went through in the previous stage and have learned to live and work better with people of a different culture. For example, in the beginning, when a Vietnamese manager first begins working in the United States, he might feel pressured and intimidated because people in the new culture are punctual in their timing when attending meetings and adhering to deadlines, compared to people at home who view time in a more relaxed manner and who work in a more laid-back style. Over time, once the timing issue has been resolved and compromise was reached, a Vietnamese manager will attune and synchronize himself towards the same "time-clock" and "time-urgency" to ensure his work is efficient and effective. Pragmatically, such an outcome transpires when the expatriate claims, "I observe, I learn, and I follow as much as I can to do the 'right' thing!"

Once an expatriate adapts, the last stage is achieving mastery through total adjustment, where the expatriate understands the new culture and eventually feels "at home." At this end of the journey, the expatriate has become acculturated to the way things are practiced in the workplace, the way people greet and communicate with each other, the way teams make decisions, the manners with which negotiation takes place and the strategies employed during conflicts. Although some of the practices, values and attitudes may not be totally consistent with those of the expat, over time, he or she grows to appreciate diverse cultural values, and consequently learns the reasons behind such behaviours, which makes them tolerable and acceptable.

There are many more challenges ahead, and I am better prepared to overcome the hurdles because I have learned the ropes of my new organizational culture, I have learned to handle my students (my dear students, to whom I feel closely connected!) and I am enjoying every bit of living in Dubai. In my opinion, being an expatriate is actually a cycle. Once you have gotten through the irritation period, then gradually adjusted, then acculturated, then you go back to the first phase of seeing everything as pleasant and wonderful – honeymooning. If the pain persists, you eventually accept that it is just part of life. No human being is without problems, and an expatriate is no exception. The main message I want you to remember today is that we need to be aware of differences; absorb them with a high degree of tolerance, acceptance and appreciation; and then act accordingly so that blunders can be lessened, if not entirely eliminated.

In a nutshell, whether one falls under the category of organizational or self-initiated expatriate, the process of cultural adjustment will naturally impact the expatriation process. All expatriate executives will experience the four stages of adjustment, with overall success contingent on factors such as previous experience living in a foreign country, length of the expatriate assignment, types of training offered prior to and during the expatriations, physical and emotional support from family and organizations, and language proficiency. What also makes a difference is how the expatriate learns to overcome his or her anxiety during the culture shock process and the steps taken to adjust to and become familiar with the new place and ways of doing things. The whole process can also be mapped against the motivation to be an expatriate, which may depend on whether he or she has moved out of willingness or has been assigned. The key question is: Do SIEs have an easier time relocating? The process will be more challenging as compared to organizational assigned expatriates because they do not have any predeparture cross-cultural training.

CULTURAL REFLECTION 3.1: GOODNESS, HOW DO I BEGIN TO PREPARE?

Nelly Orumasewe was asked by her cousin, who is working in Saudi Arabia, whether she would be interested in working as a nurse for several years in Jeddah. Nelly has just achieved her confirmation in her current position as registered nurse in a Nigerian public hospital. She has enjoyed working in Nerema Hospital for the past five years. She is excited about the idea of working abroad, yet does not know how to tell her nice and kind boss about her desire to work elsewhere. Four weeks after her interview with the hospital in Jeddah, her cousin called to happily announce that she was successful in her interview. She got the job! Suddenly, Nelly is confused, with hundreds of questions running through her mind:

- If you were Nelly, what sort of things would you want to know as an expatriate?
- What are the benefits would Nelly receive as an expatriate?
- What are the difficulties might she face working in Jeddah?
- How would Nelly assess the risks and weigh the uncertainties against the new work conditions?

CULTURAL REFLECTION 3.2: INDEED, THE HONEYMOON-ING IS OVER!

A "honeymoon stage" is a stage to which expatriates often look forward when they make the decision to move into a new environment, be it for the living or working conditions. Based on the blog vignette on the honeymoon stage by Rhea, please reflect on the following:

- What are your feelings when you undergo the honeymoon stage? Can you relate your experience using the "cultural adjustment" model (Figure 3.1)?
- Why do you think Rhea is frustrated and not able to tolerate the cultural values which are different from hers?
- How would you advise her to cope with the uncertainties of culture when it hits her, and how would she obtain mastery of the values which are inherent to her?

3.2 @CULTURAL PONDERS

Honeymooning, a Short-Shrift Moment Only!

Erzhan Raikhan
Autumn 2010

As many expatriates feel, I had the same "honeymoon" feelings coming to Dubai. Dubai, as I have mentioned in my reflective paper, is not an unknown place for me. In the past, I have travelled to Dubai as a tourist in the winter season for couple of weeks. Yet, staying as a tourist and living in a host country are completely different as you observe more events and experience numerous situations since you are now become an expatriate. Every different environment brings you to experience culture shock since the host culture is not the same as your home country's culture. For quite a period of time, in particular, I could not adapt to the weather conditions: the intense heat, especially during summer, with its high humidity level. I was missing all "the smell of air, trees, after rain," as Sayakha accurately mentioned in her blog (i.e., we have four seasons in Kyrgyzstan). After staying for quite some time here, I started to realize the big differences between here and my country (different ways of communication, etc.) and started feeling "homesick." I missed my daughter, family and friends. I realized that we are expatriates and we come here to work for a period of time, but one day, we'll go back to our countries. However, the effect of being "homesick" is reduced as I try to adjust to the new environment: I make friends with my internship colleagues and university students and we spent time outside such as going to cinemas and cafes, on trips, and so on. What I learned what that the only way to adapt to a new environment is by making friends and knowing people from the host country, where they'll make it easy for you to adapt to the country in all the ways (culture, way of living, communication, etc.). In addition to that, having a positive mindset to adapt to the new environment is advantageous. You need to surround yourself within the culture, especially if you have positive thoughts about the people here since it is a global environment. You also need to learn to adjust to different things that take place and have a strong desire to change so that, to some extent, you can be culturally competent. And I know when I reach the last stage called "biculturalism," I will learn almost all the things here in Dubai without forgetting my cultural roots!

4

The Power of Cultural Reflection

The way we experience the world around us is as a direct reflection of the world within us.

Gabrielle Bernstein

BLOG VIGNETTE 4.1 Knowing You, Knowing Me – Self-Reflection through Culture

How do you make sense of culture? What does culture mean to you? How, if at all, does culture influence your expatriation journey? In what ways, if any, is culture able to transform your life? How do you make sense of your culture, the cultural values that influence your life, and the effects of culture on your work? Undeniably, relocating or transferring to a new workplace and moving to a different country that is located far from home can be an exhilarating yet simultaneously intimidating experience. Essentially, the complex questions faced by self-initiated expatriates as they embark on their new cultural expeditions comprise the *what, why, when, who, where* and *how* of the effects of culture when entering a new environment. Some SIEs might blissfully announce, "Unfamiliar faces, different systems and a fresh environment! This is the kind of challenge I am looking for!" However, others might be distressed because of the strangeness and new ways of life. The latter individuals might also cringe upon realising that they must experience cultural shocks in the early phase of adjustment and endure a significant degree of emotional upheaval. Whilst some individuals are able to readily accept the changes they face in such situations, others take time to grasp the newness of their situations in terms of their work specifically and their lives more generally. Culture is complex and multifaceted, affects each individual in a different manner and has consequences of differing degrees. Some individuals will be energised by the exposure to a new culture and embrace it enthusiastically, while others might be perplexed and confused.

CULTURAL LESSON 4.1: CULTURAL CROSSROADS – THE VALUE OF AND NEED FOR REFLECTION

Culture represents a crossroads for countless expatriates, who are facing different cultural values, beliefs, attitudes, perceptions and behaviours in the new location. To fully appreciate new culture and gauge its impact, expatriates need to be able to reflect on and make sense of the journeys that they have experienced. Why does an individual need to engage in reflective practices? More specifically, why do SIEs who embark on cultural expeditions need to engage in reflection? Additionally, how should they reflect? The practice of reflection entails examining one's past actions with a view to engaging in a continuous process of learning, and the main aim of reflective practice in a group setting is to learn from each other. For instance, a team member who has been affected by a similar experience might be able to provide insights into how expatriates can work effectively with others.

In his classic book *Learning by Doing: A Guide to Teaching and Learning Methods*, Gibbs (1988) introduced the concept of reflective practice that enables an individual to undergo a process of examining him- or herself in depth and contemplating past events that have affected his or her life. For SIEs, the ability to explore and understand the situations that they have experienced enables them to be critical of the issues that matter when they initially enter a new environment, encounter new situations, and meet people whose behaviours and perceptions differ from their own. Additionally, this approach is a powerful way to navigate the cultural adjustment journey, as it imparts numerous *lessons to learn* on how to progress in the new culture.

Reflection can be defined in two key ways. First, reflection means engaging in deep, meaningful thought or consideration. This consideration could arise from a situation that a person has experienced in the past which has favourable or unfavourable consequences on the actions to be taken. Putting this into context, the expatriate needs to think carefully about what he or she has endured during the journey from point A to Z – that is, the good, joyful, interesting and thought-provoking experiences, as well as the bad, painful, disheartening and discouraging ones. Second, a reflection is an image seen in a mirror. The mirror enables the image to be bounced back to the individual. This definition provides insights into the ways in which an expatriate resolves the cultural dilemmas that he or she faces. Reflection can be considered an effective approach to seeing others more closely in the mirror in which one sees the reflection of oneself.

According to Trompenaars and Hampden-Turner (1997, p. 6), "Culture is the way in which a group of people solves problems and reconciles dilemmas." Individuals will always attempt to understand others and their problematic situations in light of their own mental models and perceptions; therefore, culturally reflective practices are important for SIEs, as they facilitate their exploration and understanding of each challenging phase of the adjustment process. The following discussions centre on two cultural reflection models which led to the building of a cross-cultural competency framework whose application to the SIEs' cross-cultural adjustment process is useful.

CULTURAL LESSON 4.2: CULTURAL REFLECTIONS USING THE ONION MODEL

Using the metaphor of the onion (see Figure 4.1), Hofstede (1984) and Schein (1984) introduced a model to explain culture. The following characteristics of this model explain the complexities of culture:

- The onion metaphor is based on a multilayered concept that is represented by the outermost to the innermost layers, which are found at the core of the onion.
- There are three distinct and in-depth layers represented within the onion – symbols; norms, values and behaviours; and beliefs and basic assumptions.
- Based on the first three layers, an individual can be trained in and learn about the practices that are rooted in a unique manner within a culture; however, training an individual to emulate the core values of a culture is challenging.
- The outer layer of culture is visible, while the inner layer is invisible; hence, once the onion is cut, the culture becomes visible, transparent and known.

An onion symbolises a multilayered aspect of a culture. Based on its outer layer – that is, the reddish, pinkish or purplish skin – the onion looks beautiful in the eye of the expatriates, and is, therefore, acceptable. However, a quick glance at the outer layer can sometimes be deceiving, as this does not enable one to know the condition of the onion – that is, whether it is good or rotten on the inside. The colour of the skin may also differ based on the onion's origin. Putting this into context, the onion's colour variations symbolise how people's attitudes, values, perceptions and behaviours differ depending on their culture. Nevertheless, peeling the onion's skin brings out its layers one by one, enabling the individual to begin unpacking and discovering the mysterious effects that the act of peeling brings to the surface. Once the onion is cut, there are three basic layers that signify cultural understanding.

Layer 1. The Surface and Observation Level: Signs, Artefacts and Symbols

The outer layer of an onion is called the *observation level*. This is the beginning of the thought-process, or reflective, level. Making sense of a culture requires

Outer layer: the skin of an onion

LAYER ONE : THE OBSERVATION LEVEL
Signs, Symbols & Artefacts,

Things are most visible to the eye, easily recognizable but perhaps not easy to make sense of the reasons behind it. At this level people can also see culture in a noticeable way and explicit manner. Example: Food, clothing, architecture, gestures and etc.

Middle Layer:
Start peeling the onion to discover about culture

LAYER TWO :
THE MANIFESTATION LEVEL
Norms, Traditions, Values, and Beliefs

People begin to make sense of the things or behaviors that they observe. Norms and traditions provide external pattern of behaviors which evokes feelings of appreciation. Furthermore, once people begin to accept and appreciate norms and traditions, they will develop strong cultural values and beliefs (internally driven).
Examples: Decision making process, negotiation patterns, communication style, leadership behaviors, and etc.

Core of Culture:
Look into the most inner layer of the onion"

LAYER THREE :
THE INDOCTRINATION LEVEL
Underlying Basic Assumptions

As people learn more about cultural values and beliefs, they begin to uncover implicit culture through underlying basic assumptions. Cultural theories will further help to explain the values as observed in people's behaviors. Also, rules are indoctrinated among people so that beliefs are reinforced through concrete sets of behaviors.

FIGURE 4.1

Using the onion model for reflection and cultural sense making. (From Hofstede, G. 1984. *Culture's Consequences: International Differences in Work-Related Values*. Sage Publication Inc, Newbury Park, CA; Schein, E. 1984. *Sloan Management Review*, 25(2), 3–16.)

the individual within it to be alert and to engage in sensorlike behaviour while observing the surroundings in the initial moments or phase of experiencing it; this is referred to as the honeymoon stage. When expatriates first arrive in the host country, they are surrounded by artefacts, objects and rituals which symbolise the culture in which they will now be embedded. The only way in which an expatriate will see the artefacts or symbols which inform him or her about a particular culture is through observation.

The following becomes the key question: To what extent does he or she find meaning by observing the surrounding artefacts, objects and rituals? The expatriate will have mixed feelings; it is not always easy to make sense of one's surroundings using mere observation. However, these observations which constitute collected information enable an initial interpretation, as well as an exploration of how and why the culture is different from what he or she is accustomed to. He or she should view it as an experience and an opportunity to be educated about a different culture. Thus, once an expatriate is able to make sense of an experience, he or she will be able to reflect on it. After reflection on the situation, cultural sensemaking comes to fruition.

For example, when travellers land at the international airport in Riyadh, they see only male immigration officers, who are dressed in traditional attire called a *thawb*. This well-designed, ankle-length white dress is worn by the males in the country almost like a uniform. In Dubai, the same attire, albeit with a slightly different design, is called a *kandura*. Every male worker at the Riyadh airport's immigration counter dresses in the same style. The ladies wear a long black dress, a cloak, a robelike dress known as an *abaya*, and a headscarf called a *hijab*, which all women are required to wear at work. A newly arrived expatriate might be uncertain why, based on the colours and design of the clothing, it seems as if all working men and women wear uniforms. He or she will also notice that all the people at the airport are dressed the same way. As long as the people are locals or expatriates working in the immigration office, their attire is identical. This unique clothing culture is a symbol in and of itself. It is unusual to encounter anyone who is dressed in a different colour or style. Different colours and forms of attire are evident among foreigners only.

For the most part, women who are well educated in regard to culture normally wear the *abaya* as they enter Saudi Arabia. The expatriates will search for information about what is appropriate for dressing before they enter Saudi Arabia. They might be informed during predeparture cultural training that they need to be dressed decently when they arrive in Riyadh, or they might be informed by their friends, colleagues or family members who have experienced living in the country. On the surface – the artefacts level – that is, thawb or abaya as examples of customary clothing, represents and symbolises the Arabic culture.

Once the expatriate has observed the symbols during the initial stage of learning about the culture, he or she might conclude that Saudi women wear black and the men wear white. Inadvertently, one can see cultural artefacts at the surface level only. Unfortunately, one might not fully understand the values, beliefs and reasons behind the immigration officers' traditional clothing in a uniform colour – black or white. An individual might merely see a situation or observe a person's behaviour at the surface level, and all that he or she knows is what can be seen.

Layer 2. The Manifestation Level: Feelings, Norms, Values and Behaviours

Norms inform us about how people routinely carry out tasks. Societal norms are usually shared in a society, and when all people subscribe to a common set of norms and values, this is called culture. The second layer is called the *manifestation level*. Once the individual cuts and begins to peel away the layers of the onion by making further enquiries about the surrounding people, he or she will begin to understand the reasons for the colour and design of the *abaya* or *thawb*. By engaging in conversations with friends and colleagues, he or she might begin to explore information and seek explanations regarding the design of the clothing. The individual can then begin to uncover the meaning and value of modesty in terms of fashion/design and colour in light of Islamic culture.

For Islamic women, modesty in regard to dress is the key factor determining why their black garments are long and provide proper coverage of certain parts of the body, such as the neck, arms and legs. If the individual is curious, he or she might pose a question that is rooted in curiosity about the local culture: Should the *abaya* always be black? If so, why are no other colours allowed? Which is more significant in terms of religious values – colour or design? Islamic law, which is the basis of religious values with regard to clothing, emphasises three principles: modesty, decency and respect. Women should, therefore, choose their attire carefully based on these criteria. However, the colour black has been accepted by women for many generations, as there are practices that are passed down through society. As such, to some extent, it becomes second nature for women to wear black *abayas*. However, over time, the design and colour of *abayas* have changed. In Dubai, for example, various designers have created a new type of *abaya*. Nevertheless, although they are in line with the modern world in terms of contemporary designs, colours and fabrics, they retain the cultural values of modesty, decency and respect. In this regard, therefore, the norms are maintained. Being knowledgeable of such changes when they take place allows an individual to understand the uniqueness of societal and cultural needs.

Layer 3. The Indoctrination Level: Beliefs and Basic Assumptions

The third or innermost layer of the onion model is the indoctrination level. Indoctrination is the process of inculcating ideas, beliefs, attitudes and strategies. In short, it refers to instilling the know-how to respond to the cultural dilemmas that are faced in the workplace and in life more generally. As the individual further penetrates the multiple layers of explanations to enable understanding of the cultural nuances of another person, he or she also begins to understand that this person's beliefs and observed behaviours will result in concrete assumptions about the person who is being observed.

Human behaviour is embedded and manifested in a cultural context. One has to undertake an in-depth exploration of cultural assumptions by looking through a theoretical lens, thereby enabling engagement in cultural sensemaking. From childhood through to adulthood, culture is formed, learned and passed down through generations within context. For example, at an early age, an individual is indoctrinated by the parent–child relationship, which is shaped primarily by the parent. As a result of this lengthy learning process, the learned values will be accumulated and then shared as people go out into the society – that is, at school and then in the workplace during adulthood.

The person who reaches this innermost layer will begin to unravel and reveal a covert aspect of a culture – the dos and don'ts and the underlying basic assumptions which offer explanations about the values and behaviours. In keeping with my previous clothing example – that is, knowing that the reason for wearing the *abaya* is rooted in Islamic values – one will begin to understand the beliefs, behaviours and mindsets of the person who is being immersed in a new culture, known as cultural recipients. The individual's curiosity will be assuaged, and rules will become known and crystallised.

Our lives are guided by rules that provide us with a *way of doing things*. In other words, people need guidelines that help to direct us in terms of how to carry out tasks. In fact, culture is a way of life, and so are Islamic values. Our beliefs and basic assumptions provide a clear understanding of our core values. A value can be defined as conviction in the form of beliefs, faith or principles deemed valuable to someone, which provides meaning to a person. An individual who is without values will have no direction in life, as they indicate the ways in which people should operate on a daily basis whether at work or in life in general.

Therefore, to uncover the core meaning of the values underlying manifested behaviours, it is necessary to use a theoretical lens to provide descriptions and explanations of the why, when, who and how of people's thoughts, feelings and actions. Wearing an *abaya*, for example, is prescribed by the Islamic values of modesty, decency and respect. The choice of colour is largely dependent on the cultural norms of the relevant society. Until decades ago, in numerous Arabic countries, one colour, black, was used for clothing.

However, in the current fashion design and clothing market, the customary black colour of the *abaya* is slowly being changed. Fashion designers are introducing other colours, tones and shades while still retaining the core Islamic values of decency, modesty and respect. As long as the clothing provides full coverage and protection of certain important parts of the body in compliance with Islamic law, the basic rules and cultural assumptions are considered to be aligned with cultural values.

Expatriates must reflect extensively on the cultural values that affect them during the adjustment phase. It is important to determine the appropriate behaviours in which to engage. However, it is not easy to uncover these cultural values and practices, unless the expatriate undergoes the experience while having well-informed knowledge and receiving appropriate advice. An individual's mental models and perceptions must change if he or she is to accommodate new cultural knowledge. In other words, indoctrination needs to take place, as knowledge of the rules and general ways of doing things paves the way to better adjustment strategies. Support, including from colleagues, spouses and family members, must be available and reliable to provide guidance in the right direction. Basic cultural assumptions, rules and guidelines need to be effectively shared, disseminated more widely and passed on to the expatriates so that they do not make cultural blunders.

Given the case of the *abaya*, women entering Saudi Arabia should understand the value of dressing modestly. They should appreciate the dress code and accept the underlying reasons for such attire. Although this example pertains to the external aspect of a culture – known as the tangible or material culture – it enables a realisation of how culture shapes one's internal values and behaviours, which should be consistent in regard to their alignment with the society in which an individual resides.

CULTURAL LESSON 4.3: USING THE CYCLE OF REFLECTION TO UNDERSTAND THE CULTURAL EXPERIENCE

Gibbs (1988) introduced the cycle of reflection to affirm that human beings learn better through the lens of experience. His research is grounded in the early work on the experiential learning process, proposed by Kolb (1984), who identified four types of learner behaviours. Let us examine the cycle of reflective practice (see Figure 4.2) to enable a complete understanding of the process of reflection. An individual undergoes five basic stages that occur in a cyclic manner that is both interactive and iterative. Gibb's model

FIGURE 4.2
Reflective practices cycle. (From Gibbs, G. 1988. *Learning by Doing: A Guide to Teaching and Learning Methods*. Further Education Unit. Oxford: Oxford Polytechnic.)

promotes repetition – that is, repeating the understanding of culture. In this case, we are referring to expatriates' knowledge and sensemaking with regard to the cultural values that are embedded in the situations that they encounter. They cannot understand cultural assumptions by merely observing artefacts; rather, they must interact with others and the environment to enable them to accurately interpret the culture. The following are the six key stages of this process.

Stage 1. Description of the Occurrence: What Happened?

The key issue at this stage relates to identifying the meaning of culture by making sense of the reality or event. This enables the individual to identify what is happening or has happened by describing the event; however, it is not easy to describe the event unless he or she is not only observant but also intrigued by it. The following question should be asked at this stage: What is happening or has transpired? The sensemaking exercise for the expatriate entails trying his or her best to describe the event in extensive detail. It could also be an act whereby the expatriate identifies the root cause of the event by unpacking its elements and characteristics to find meaning.

Stage 2. Emotions and Reactions: What Were the Person's Feelings, and How Did He or She React?

At this stage, the expatriate will begin to figure out his or her feelings. He or she will be able to understand the event from an emotional standpoint and have a deeper feeling or sensory experience (than during the first stage) regarding why an event or situation occurred. It is also important to understand one's reaction to such an event.

Stage 3. Evaluation

During the evaluative stage, the expatriate will deepen his or her understanding of the situation by asking a key question: What was positive or negative about the experience? It is important for him or her to acknowledge these feelings by rationalising and thinking logically, and to evaluate by making sense of the situation. In other words, when an event or situation occurs, an individual needs to look at it in an objective manner, describe the event based on value evaluation, and acquire an in-depth understanding of the manifested behaviours.

Stage 4. Analysis

To make sense of culture, expatriates need to think analytically. At this stage, they can fully diagnose and then create certain culturally attuned conditional rules regarding their own behaviour. Once an expatriate evaluates a situation that has triggered certain reactions, he or she needs to then analyse it through various theoretical lenses. Cultural theories offer descriptions about a phenomenon, enable the understanding of key factors that impact behaviours, and explain a situation or the shared values that are inherent in a society. Prescriptions in the form of cultural doctrines are a useful outcome of understanding the behaviours which ensures that people are guided by cultural conditions. Consequently, this allows expatriates to understand which norms are accepted and which are not.

Stage 5. Conclusion

At this stage, the following key question arises: What else could have been done? The expatriates take a reflective approach that involves questioning which feelings and behaviours could have moulded them in a different way. They need to take a step back and critically examine the what, why, when, who, where and how of the situations that they have experienced and contemplate whether they could have turned out differently. The question essentially asks how behaving differently could potentially lead to different outcomes. This is an important aspect of reflection, as it constitutes solution-based thinking, which leads to the next and final stage.

Stage 6. Action Plan

During this final stage, the expatriate can formulate his or her strategic and solution-based plans. All the factors which either inhibit or facilitate his or her cultural actions and reactions need to be taken into consideration. The process comes to an end by examining the responses to the following instrumental enquiry: If and when a situation recurs, how would he or she react, or what would he or she do differently? At this stage, the expatriate is expected to identify the cultural blunders that were made during the early stage of adjustment. The so-called culture shock stages are a good place to begin the reflection exercise because they address the conflicts and turbulence that were experienced, and it is critical to be able to make sense of such experiences. Expatriates also need to reflect on the positive experiences, formulate balanced strategies in light of the pros and cons of the situations they have encountered, and consequently develop strategic and culturally acceptable action plans.

CULTURAL LESSON 4.4: WHY IS REFLECTION NECESSARY?

One needs to look back, ponder what has happened and contemplate the numerous anguished and gratifying moments in one's life. Likewise, expatriates need to reflect on the journey – that is, the cross-cultural adjustment expedition – that they have undertaken. If an individual goes through life without engaging in some degree of sensemaking, he or she will be somewhat oblivious to the unexplainable aspects of his or her past experiences. As SIEs, some crucial questions will run through your mind:

- How can I be well informed and educated about the next step forward?
- How can I be sensitive to the emotions that I have experienced?
- How should I react to events and mould my behaviours in a manner that is congruent with cultural values of the host country?

If an expatriate fail to reflect deeply by making sense of his or her cultural experiences, such encounters will not be translated into lessons learned, which makes up important information that should be communicated to newly arrived SIEs.

According to Gibbs (1988), the purpose of engaging in reflective practices is to question assumptions and explanations, seek different ways of knowing through the exploration of ideas and strategies, enhance self-awareness and self-development by taking action as problem-solvers, and integrate theories with practice. Gibbs vehemently promoted learning by doing and argued that theory without practice is inconceivable. The key advantages of reflection include the following:

- The ability to look into oneself and others, as it is about knowing the unknowns.
- The ability to realise what works and transpires effectively in the culture one experiences.
- The ability to acknowledge why and when cultural blunders are made.

- The ability to rectify mistakes as soon as they occur.
- The ability to become sensitised to one's surroundings and the cultural nuisance that these create.
- The ability to defend oneself from cultural hostility.
- The ability to avoid engaging in cultural stereotyping.
- The ability to persevere when it comes to understanding the complexity of behaviours by examining them through a cultural lens.

CULTURAL REFLECTION 4.1: SILENCE IS POWERFUL, UNDENIABLY!

Mariah Thomas did not know why things had happened the way they had. She faced a perplexing dilemma: How would she deal with the silence of her supplier in India? As an expatriate sales and marketing manager in Bangkok, Mariah had to deal with Manush Mohan, an operations and logistics senior manager in Mumbai. One day, she contacted him regarding a missed deadline. She requested detailed information regarding the delayed shipment and demanded a speedy explanation. As she began the conversation, she immediately blurted, "Manush, why did the shipment to Chicago get stranded? It was delayed for over six days, and the customer is extremely unhappy. I owe him an explanation immediately, as the delay is costly!" Her direct and aggressive tone seemed to evoke an unpleasant feeling of indifference within Manush. However, his immediate reaction was "I apologise, Mariah. I will see what I can do to rectify this situation." This conversation was followed by a week of no contact with Manush. Waiting impatiently, Mariah was uncertain how to proceed. She had made two phone calls and sent two emails to Manush over the past five days but had received no return calls or messages. In retrospect, Mariah needed to reflect on this cultural scenario. In essence, what cultural blunder had occurred?

In regard to the case above, the reflective practice can be approached in two distinct ways:

Reflection in action – interaction with the current event as it evolves or transpires

- Can you describe the experience between Manush vs. Mariah?
- What are your thoughts during the event?

- What are your reactions as the problem or event unfolds?
- Are your actions immediate or delayed?

Reflection on action – describing the process of reflection which takes place after the event

- Do you think of the kinds of action you should have taken?
- Would you do anything differently? If yes, can you explain how your actions would be different?
- What are some of the explanations you can offer based on the case of Mariah and Manush? Are there any theoretical explanations to help anchor such an event based on meaningful interpretations?
- How do you process your feelings and actions?

CULTURAL REFLECTION 4.2: RECOUNT THE CULTURAL EXPERIENCE

Think of a situation that you have experienced as an expatriate. Recount the moment you first experienced a new culture in a host country.

- What were your thoughts and perceptions of that particular moment, having just arrived from your home country?
- How do you feel in a foreign workplace, where things are new and strange?
- Why did you act or react to certain situations the way you did?

Based on these three anchor questions, look back at a specific situation that had culturally rich aspects. Using the template from Gibbs' model, let us engage in a cycle of reflective practice. Below is a form that asks key questions that are used to conduct a reflective cultural exercise. Please note that the questions listed under the six stages are not exhaustive. Some may be relevant to your context, while some may not. Choose the ones that you find relatable, and then reflect on the selected situation. Input your thoughts, feelings and actions in the blank space under Table 4.1.

TABLE 4.1

Reflective Logs and Exercise

Stages	Goals	Reflective Questions	Your Own Reflection
1. Description	To be able to identify and describe an experience pertaining to a culturally rooted incident/situation. • This is at the descriptive (not analytical) level.	• What happened? • Why did it happen? • Where and when did it happen? • Who was affected by the occurrence? • How did it come about?	

2. Feelings	To be able to describe the feelings related to the incident
	• This is the description of feelings and the reactions to what transpired. It is not analytical in nature.
	• Answer only those questions that are relevant to your context and experience.
		• How did you feel when the incident occurred?
		  • How did you feel prior to the incident?
		  • How did you feel during that incident?
		• How did you react when you experienced the incident?
		• How did you feel after the incident? What did you think?	

3. Evaluation	To be able to make a judgment, whether positive or negative, about an experience. • Choose only one or two incidents at a time to enable effective reflection. • Choose the incidents that are most relevant to and representative of the experience.	• What went well during the incident? • What went wrong during the incident? • How was the situation remedied? Was there any compromise, solution or resolution? • Did you complete the cycle of cultural experience despite the mistakes made?	
4. Analysis	To be able to develop analytical thinking skills to enable a thorough examination of the situation at hand. • Try to explain the cause and effect relationship of the occurrence. • Seek to answer critical questions (e.g., why, so what and what if …).	• Reconsider what went well, and write why you think it went well or why you think it was unsuccessful. • Reconsider the things that went badly and write what you think led to the consequences of the action.	

(Continued)

TABLE 4.1 (*Continued*)

Reflective Logs and Exercise

Stages	Goals	Reflective Questions	Your Own Reflection
		• Think about what could have been done to have avoided these negative consequences. • Reconsider the things that went well and write why you think they went well. • Reconsider the things that went well and write what you think led to these consequences of the action.	
5. Conclusion	To be able to summarise what was learnt and derive knowledge from the experience. • Try to be specific or elaborate on specific things you have learned or realised. • Discover previously unknown aspects of yourself.	• What should or could I have done differently? • What stopped me from doing this? • What did I learn about myself during the experience (positive and/or negative)? • What did I learn about my current knowledge or level of practice (strengths and weaknesses)? • Did the experience achieve any of my learning goals or meet any of my required competencies?	
6. Action Plan	To be able to provide comprehensive plans to move forward in terms of settling into the new culture, as well as justification and value for the actions to be taken. • Aim to provide action-oriented statements to improve knowledge, ability and cultural experiences. • Indicate the specific training programs, policy guidelines and resources to be used.	• What do I need to do in order to be better prepared to face this experience in future? • Even if the experience was positive and I did well, in which areas can I improve? • What are the priority areas that need to be developed? • What specific steps do I need to take in order to achieve these improvements?	

Source: Gibbs, G. 1988. *Learning by Doing: A Guide to Teaching and Learning Methods.* Further Education Unit. Oxford: Oxford Polytechnic.

Note: Key in your own observations as frequently as possible.

4.1 @CULTURAL PONDERS

Sure, No Words Needed, He Knows and Understands!

Hela Al Murad

Autumn 2010

Last week, I was reading a journal on Hall's theory of high-context and low-context people. It was very interesting that this theory explained to me many things I did and still do, referring them to my own personality. Whilst reading this journal, I understood that my personality is a manifestation of my culture. For example, when I am upset at a friend or my husband, I refuse to explain why I am upset, thinking that they are very close to me and should feel and understand me even more than I understand myself. Reading Hall's theory, I found that I come from a high-context culture in which people do not discuss embarrassing issues; they assume that they understand each other very well and keep talking around the subject without putting into words the real issue they are discussing, while people in low-context cultures can discuss any issue and put anything on the table without being shy or embarrassed. They tend to be very clear and explain everything, assuming that the other person knows nothing about them. Returning to the main subject, that is, saying NO to people, I find it difficult to do so especially when people are asking a favour as I am coming from a high-context culture. I have been raised by a mother who never shut her door or turned down people who came to her believing that she would truly help. Her best two pieces of advice were: (a) do not let down people who come to you seeking your help and believing you will help (as long as you can help) and (b) do not wait for people to thank you for what you did – do it because you know it is the right thing to do. However, working with many nationalities, especially from the West, has made me more objective and helped me to say NO if the request will harm our business or will come at the expense of our performance. But I still find it difficult to say no if the person's request comes as a favour. It is only then that I [open up] my schedule and do my best to help.

Section II

Cultural Impacts on Management Practices

5

Cross-Cultural Communication

The essence of cross-cultural communication has more to do with releasing responses than with sending messages. It is more important to release the right response than to send the message.

Edward T. Hall

BLOG VIGNETTE 5.1   Mind Your Language, Please!

A few years ago, I worked with an American managing editor whom I emailed back and forth several times at the inception stage of our ephemeral collaboration before my article was published. One day, in one of our many emails, I was taken aback when the editor blurted the following: "I tried many times to find your personal information, but your damn website made it so difficult for me to do so!" I understood this person was trying to express his frustrations and anger over an important matter, that is, accessing appropriate information to publish my article within an urgent timeline. I instantly wanted to tell him, "Hey, watch your language!" Instead, I said, "You don't have to get mad over it." I think that remark got him to realise that his reaction wasn't right. After that incident, I thought of the different communication styles people use in relating their frustrations. My question is: When and in what manner could we teach people to do it our way? Why and with whom would a person learn to be polite and cautious with one's words? Could or would people simply say what and how they want by employing an authentic approach and a customary way of speaking?

CULTURAL LESSON 5.1: COMMUNICATE THE RIGHT MANNER, PLEASE

Communication is crucial; so is one's attitude. Respecting others and having high tolerance are needed when you work with someone who has different cultural values. To the managing editor, perhaps the statement was simply an expression of feelings. To me, it represented his level of tolerance and respect. Whether people say what they mean or mean what they say, it all boils down to the way a person thinks and feels about a situation. To me, saying something invokes the necessity of contemplating the effect it will cause on others, which is indeed a priority over my own feelings, sometimes even at the expense of bottling up my feelings. Justifiably, I witness this passive communication style in people who ascribe to a collectivistic culture. Given a certain context, in specific situations, they also employ a nonconfrontational approach and avoidance strategy of communication. How would Westerners employ a direct, confrontational strategy in response to this conflicting manner?

According to Hall (1976), the founder of the intercultural communication field, communication is culture, and culture is communication. On the contrary, behaviour under the abovementioned illustration can also be attributed to one's personality. I do realise that it is not right to say all Americans are blunt and harsh. Some of the Americans I know seem politer than my own people back home in Malaysia. And there are Asians, after all, who are loud and nasty in their speech. When we say "culture," we mean we observe many, many people who practise in such a way, validating our observations with evidence. Of course, it all depends on situational conditions. As I was reading an article on managerial skills and negotiation that addresses authority and power, I thought:

- How do people communicate with their superiors, that is, their bosses or colleagues?
- More specifically, how does one say "no" to their boss or colleague?
- Is it a common practice? It depends.

Many people have different ways of communicating a decision like "no." Some may use the word bluntly and straightforwardly. For instance, one time my European colleague came to the meeting, listened and then announced to the Dean: "I don't agree with the idea and will not carry out the task because I don't see that it is feasible." Meanwhile, one of my Asian colleagues just nodded and supported the statement with a subtle and polite manner. Another colleague began to utter his disagreement with such a statement: "I am sorry, I do agree with Frank on the unfeasibility of the task, and I think it is better for us to carry out the task this way …," while others just stared blankly and refused to utter any words. For many, saying "no" is not easy. In some cultures, saying no is not a big deal. You do it with ease, you do it without guilt and you do it all the time.

But in other cultures, saying "no" is a "no-no." You do what you are told, whether you are willing or not. You perform the task because you respect the authority of the person who requests or instructs it. So, the communication style in both scenarios is different. In a culture when saying "no" is easy and acceptable, communicating a negative response is no problem. In a culture where saying "no" is hard and usually unacceptable, communication can come in two forms: verbal or nonverbal. For instance, when an employee does not want to do what he or she is asked, the boss can see this through his or her facial expressions, such as a confused or hesitant look or a frown. A lagging or slow response can also be a cue.

Yet, this type of communication is subtle: It takes experience and intimacy to understand the level of another's willingness without him or her saying yes or no concretely. The opposite is true for the low-context culture communicator where they can express their feelings by straightforwardly saying No. People from this culture can offer a negative response verbally without remorse. They can say no to you blankly, with a straight face. Sometimes, this is communicated in a very diplomatic and professional way. However, it is said, it will be communicated directly.

**BLOG VIGNETTE 5.2   Why Should It Be Different?
Communicating at Home and at Work**

Over the years, I have been amazed at the different ways people communicate in their daily lives, especially at work. I wonder whether *what and how* you were taught to communicate at home affects how you speak in the workplace, and whether how you speak at work influences how you speak to your spouse and kids at home. A friend of mine once told me that her husband speaks to her as if she is a member of his staff – the "boss" tone, she said. Another friend shared with me a piece of her work wisdom: "I have developed a diplomatic way to communicate with my staff. When there's a problem, I call them and ask them directly what problems they are facing, and then reason the issues out with them. The funny part is that when speaking to my kids, I began to use the same communication style. Strangely it worked!" These examples make it evident that people learn to communicate with co-workers based on what they are taught by their parents, siblings and friends, and vice versa. Some people might just say that it needs to be different – professionally and socially. What you say, when you deliver it, which context it exists in, with whom you are speaking, and the manner in which you deliver your speech are all crucial formations of one's communication styles. So I often ponder: Why should it be different? After all, everyone starts developing their *speaking ability* as young as one year old. From that moment onwards, one is taught and trained how to talk based on the influential people in life within the environment one is in – that is, parents, siblings, teachers and friends. Such growing years will provide a learning experience on how best to speak with other people. People and environment are two elements that will help develop a specific communication style which is attuned to your own cultural roots. So, conceivably, I suggest: speak the way you do as you are taught, and speak the way you desire as you observed! Language is cultural tool for human communication.

CULTURAL LESSON 5.2: WHAT DID YOU SAY? DIFFERENT CULTURES, DIFFERENT COMMUNICATION STYLES

From a cultural point of view, there are many differences in the ways people speak, including the way people *arrange* their words, the *tone of voice* they use, how they select the *content* of a message, and the person to whom they direct the message. Studies have shown that culture does influence communication. Edward Hall's (1959) intercultural communication theory introduced a concept called "context" as a way to explain communicative behaviour. This concept refers to the extent to which communication is affected by its context (the situation) vs. content (the words). Context is a continuum with two extremes, high and low. Communication in a high-context society takes into consideration key factors such as what, who, why, when and how. On the other hand, communication in a low-context society relies almost exclusively on what – that is, the content of the message. Thus, in a low-context culture, people directly express their disagreement, while in a high-context culture, people are reluctant to speak if they fear they will offend someone (their boss, for example, or their father). In that sense, it is true, as Edward Hall asserted, that culture is communication and communication is culture. High-context cultures are from countries like those in Asia, that is, Japan, Malaysia, Thailand, China and India; South American countries like Brazil; and most of the Middle Eastern countries like Saudi Arabia, United Arab Emirates, Iran, Egypt and many others. On the other hand, low-context cultures include countries like the United States and Anglo-Saxon cultures like Germany, Australia, Netherlands, Norway, Denmark, Finland, United Kingdom, Canada and Sweden, among others.

So, when working with people from different cultures, you need to be aware of their various *communicative behaviours*, because any blunders in conversation will lead to miscommunication, misinterpretations or confusion, all of which can adversely affect performance. In a nutshell, "What did you say?" not only matters, but also "What did you not say?" is equally important. Through his research, Hall found that, in certain cultures, people use something called *silent language*. Silent language is as powerful as *uttered language*: what a person doesn't say may give a very different meaning to the message, and the message may therefore be misunderstood by people who are used to listening only to people's explicit words. A high-context culture depends heavily on nonverbal cues. Communication may employ a range of facial expressions, for example signalling agreement through a nodding of the head; a bow to show respect for the person one is communicating with; or a stare to express confusion, disagreement or disapproval. In the global workplace, particularly in global virtual teams, people communicate online, work virtually and collaborate with strangers who are separated by thousands of miles. In such an environment, people set a different tone of teamwork and communication styles. Hence, it is in your workplace that you will be given a golden opportunity to experience the different ways, mannerisms and approaches of communicating. Only you can make sense of its meaning if and when you evaluate it through a cultural lens.

CASE BLOG 5.1

Khor: Express it implicitly

When I talk with my team members, I usually express my idea implicitly. I am [from] a high-context culture. I always use euphemistic words such as "maybe" and "I guess," and I am not sure I like these words. I also often voice a positive opinion after someone had given their suggestions – I almost totally agree with their ideas. An example is our team process of selecting a marketplace. I wanted to recommend China for analysis. However, one team member was strongly opposed to my idea. I just kept silent and followed that suggestion at last. Another example situation is when I found that one member had made a mistake when she distributed tasks to other members. All I said to her was that maybe we need to confirm the instructions of the weekly survey, even though I knew she had made a mistake. For my introductory message, the reason I stated it so briefly is that I was afraid to make a bad impression on my group members. I did not know anything about them, so I tried to avoid uncertain things happening.

CASE BLOG 5.2

Arni: An assertive kind of person

I am an assertive kind of person. I tend to speak what is on my mind, without trying to underestimate and blame others for that matter. I will clearly state my opinions and feelings to people right away. I believe that if I am doing well and always respect others, people will tend to do the same towards me. So, even though I am a very straightforward kind of person, I will never ever violate the rights of others. I tend to listen to other opinions also, even if I'm giving my honest opinion to them – for me, it is a win-win situation for both parties. Instead of talking behind someone's back, I am delighted to tell them the truth and I expect people will do the same, so no one is talking behind the back of anyone. Besides, I will always maintain a good, mature tone of voice when I speak out, as it allows the discussion to stay respectful and prevents either party from being emotionally driven away if the talk is not working as planned.

CASE BLOG 5.3

Adnan: Be direct and elaborate

I have been through several levels of communication styles, I think. Before I joined Phillip Morris International, my communication style was influenced mostly by my surroundings in Malaysia, where I lived with friends from my university who were also freshly graduated with their diplomas. We rented a house in Shah Alam, Selangor, where each of us worked in different fields. My communication style was indirect, succinct and contextual. I had a tendency to always express via my facial expressions, too often be unsure of what to say, and to follow voices of the majority and just agree with people who seemed to be in charge. I experienced a culture shock in communication when I joined Phillip Morris. The working conditions required me to be more vocal and more critical in thinking. So, I have moved to a higher level of communication. Besides receiving messages via e-mails, workshops and training, I need to convey clear and precise messages to my subordinates every day. My style of communication has become more direct and elaborate. Even now, I use the same style when I communicate to my wife and daughter, my sisters and my in-laws. They now see me as a person who only talks about things that matter. And my wife has been influenced by me when she communicates to our six-year-old daughter, explaining "what" and "why" to answer her questions, and ensuring she understands the content.

BLOG VIGNETTE 5.3 A Word of Honour

One day, I wanted to borrow the *Socio-Cultural Handbook* from our library. The library staff, however, informed me that my colleague Norsaadah Hamid had also requested it. As the library only held one copy, this created a constraint for both of us. Saadah told me she needed the book only for the next couple of days, and I told her the same. After going back and forth trying to negotiate who would get it first, I compromised and set a timeline. I asked her to read it for one day and then pass it to me the next. With relief in her eyes, she held the book in the air and said,

I promise you! First thing tomorrow morning, I will return the book!

I was so occupied with my deadlines that the next day I totally forgot about the book. So, on the morning of the second day, as I was walking into the department, I went straight to Saadah's room to get the copy. After all, the book was delayed for two days now and, by right, it should be my turn. I knocked on her door and as she opened it.

I said, "Assalamualaikum, how are you?
Anyway, can I get the book?
Hmm, you said you will return to me after a day, right?"
With a guilty voice, she announced, "Sorry, I didn't even look at it yet, but I need it for another two days!"

I was upset at that time because I also needed the book urgently and I had compromised for her to use it first. Without much thought, I gave her a look of nonapproval. She then confessed to me that her deadline was actually next week. As she said,

> Initially, I thought I would prioritize that assignment. Unfortunately, I was caught up with many administrative tasks ... I am so sorry, here you can take it first.

I took the book and thanked her. Had I known that she was not in urgent need of it, I would have used the book first. As I was walking back to my office, I contemplated the incident. *Saadah had promised me, hadn't she? What was that all about?* I then reflected on my own role in the situation. Several thoughts ran through my mind: I wasn't the one who made the promise, and I certainly wasn't the one who had failed to return the book. I thought we had an agreement, I thought she understood that each of us had a deadline!

CULTURAL LESSON 5.3: I PROMISE! BUT DO YOU MEAN IT?

The words "I promise" imply various meanings in business deals and work contexts, depending on the cultural perspective. For instance, in business, when two parties negotiate and then sign a contract, the respective parties are expected to honour and comply with the agreement made. Such action implies that the parties involved will deliver what has been agreed upon based on the itemized agenda – with all the set tasks, timeline and outcomes. The bottom line is, "I promise to do this, this and this!" The contract is indicative of one's actions. In negotiations, however, two contradictory situations exist – actions based on written words or actions based on an established relationship. From a cultural point of view, the words "I promise" may be analyzed in different manners, with different meanings and in relation to different strategies. So, what do these two words mean? Several cultural dimensions can offer insight.

For example, in collectivistic cultures, such as Japan, Thailand, Malaysia, China and many other Asian countries, the negotiation process begins with listening and discussions. This process somehow unfolds into different stages of discussions, until the negotiators develop a trusting feeling towards each other. Once trust is developed, negotiation is sealed with the underlying understanding of, "I promise to do it, because we have bonded." Hence, time is essential in any communication process for a high-context and collectivist society. One needs patience and understanding: no rushing and pressuring if you want them to keep their promises. It can be an insult for them if you push the contract as the key indicator of trust. Well, it may be easy to verbalise, "I promise," but keeping it is another question. So be cautious, when someone says, "I promise."

In a society where individualism is a predominant cultural value, however, the word "promise" is verbalised through a piece of paper. Once a person signs such a document, it means that the person is endorsing the business contract. The promise is reflected in the negotiating parties' behaviours and written words. If cultural values have such a strong influence on how we make and keep promises, then how do we recognize when people break their promises when we are dealing with different cultures? For example, in an individualistic society, people are considered not to honour their promises when they breach a contract. Breaking a promise means people violate some of the principles or itemized actions stipulated in the contract. But how about people from collectivist cultures? They take the piece of paper as an initial step to a more promising behaviour. Once trust is built, only then do their behaviours truly reflect of those words, "I promise!" Try to uncover the cultural values hidden under such words, or you could be in for a surprise!

For instance, in a culture that is prescribed with religious values and practices, like the Muslim countries, the phrase "Insha'Allah," or "God willing," is supposed to express one's serious intent to complete a task. The person must do one's best and leave the rest to God, acknowledging that not everything is in his or her control. Unfortunately, the phrase is often misused, with people saying "Insha'Allah" even if they do not intend to fulfil the promise. Ahmed, a Dubai resident from Iran, describes his own mixed intentions around making promises, and explores differing uses of "Insha'Allah" which can result in more confusion and misinterpretation from people who do not completely understand the real meaning of "Insha'Allah." He said, "One should not use the word casually when he or she cannot make promises; it is confusing and misleading to other cultures!"

In the context of Dubai as an Islamic country, I appreciate the religious dimension when relating to culture. According to me, the phrase "Insha'Allah" has a very promising connotation – provided that the promise maker thoughtfully uses the expression. It felt very strange when I heard most people using the term "Insha'Allah" casually when I first came to Dubai. When I totally understood the spiritual dimension of this special word, I realized how relieved we can be when we leave it all in God's hands. This lessens the burden and stress to focus on the outcome of the promise, regardless of its realization; it's God's will, be it positive or negative. This has therefore taught me to become more patient and tolerant in life and with any individual I am confronted with. I am sure many would argue that the use of "Insha'Allah" in the Arabic culture is symbolic to delay a promise until a future time, which lengthens the procedure. Nevertheless, when the promise maker wisely uses the term "Insha'Allah," it conveys a positive approach to the receiver.

CASE BLOG 5.4

Perez: A promised culture clash

I stick to the statement that "promise" is a word that changes its meaning according to the culture as well as the situation. I would like to support this line with a real-life incident that happened to me. My roommate is from Korea. We both decided to go for exercise every day in the evening. And he made me *promise* that I would come for exercise regularly. After some days of heavy regular exercise, I decided to take a break for some days. I told my friend this and he was angry with me. He reminded me that I had "promised." Of course, I remember but, come on man, it's just exercise … and boy was he pissed with me. It was only after having a long conversation with him that I understood that, according to his culture, if someone makes a promise of something, even as informal as exercise, they have to keep the promise, or else be considered really rude. According to me, an informal promise such as the exercise can be broken when it is proved that the person tried. Anyways, I have realized that "promise" is a dangerous word that needs to be used carefully.

CASE BLOG 5.5

Ahmad: Insha'Allah

Promises can be addressed and understood in different ways, depending on the background a person comes from. As you mentioned, people will attend their promises in ways that are compatible, or we can say familiarised, with the way they lived or learned from their own culture. Usually, when I promise, I tend to keep my promise no matter what happens. On the other hand, sometimes I promise only to get rid of the person who is insisting on something from me. In addition, sometimes I promise a friend to do him/her a favour even though I know that I can't do it, only so they don't feel bad and so I can show them that I'm doing my best to keep my promise. I believe that, nowadays, people's approaches to promises are a mixture of their original culture and values, as well as those they have gained from other cultures, due to globalisation trends. This is the reason why people from the same culture may adhere to their promises differently. In other words, some people uses the sentence "Insha'Allah" to show that they are serious to deliver what they promise, and others use it to express that they will never do it.

BLOG VIGNETTE 5.4   Actions Speak Louder Than Words!

At a university I once worked at, a colleague used to say of our dean, "I wish he would just say what he means!" And my response was always, "Hasn't he said enough?" My colleague would then ask "How?" and I would say, "Don't you see it in his face?" I know for sure my former boss did not always communicate his wants directly to his subordinates. He did, however, communicate in other ways. At times, he expressed what he wanted to his deputy deans or close colleagues. At other times, while not stating what he wanted directly, he said it with a frown on his face to indicate anxiety and frustrations. At other times, he showed he was delighted by smiling and nodding his head in total agreement with our ideas! It is so difficult to read one's thoughts and feelings. Yet, coming from high-context culture, we also seem to interpret and judge others' nonverbal behaviours all the time. This made me wonder: To what extent do "actions speak louder than words," particularly in a society that is low context? In low-context societies, words need to be verbalised and/or written down (contracts). Actions can be wrongly interpreted due to lack of clarity in a document or lack of details in one's explanation. But for members of a high-context society who are totally dependent on nonverbal cues, actions and behaviours are key indicators for many aspects, such as approval or disagreement. High-context cultures search for signs and clues based on facial expressions, movement, gestures and other body language. Direct language, on the other hand, can lead to uncomfortable feelings.

CULTURAL LESSON 5.4: YOU ARE BEING TOO BLUNT, AREN'T YOU?

As a member of a high-context culture, I can relate directly to the experience of fear in the face of directness. When words are blurted right in our face, it can make us feel uncomfortable, humiliated and demotivated. Honesty and truth in this respect can even be hurtful. I used to tell my three sisters of my experience in the United States, when a person, such as a professor or colleague, would be direct with me. At that very moment I would feel like running away and hiding under the table … urrrgh, it was so embarrassing! On the other hand, someone need not say something out loud, but I will understand it instantly from an explicit display of a behaviour. I wonder if we can develop the same understanding of silence. Is silence interpretable? Can we accept silence as an effective communicative behaviour? In the past, I was a person who most of the time could not verbalise my thoughts and feelings, but rather reflected them in my face. Only recently have I become more sensitive to this. I have now learned to synchronise my nonverbal language with my verbal language so that people cannot misinterpret my messages. So, my *actions* are equivalent to my *words,* I believed. I have learned how to say "I am happy" with a light in my eyes and a smile on my face, as well as to say "I am frustrated" with a grim face.

CASE BLOG 5.6

Rehma: We have to do it … and say it

Not only do my parents come from a high-context culture, but they raised us with a great focus on what we need to do, rather than just say. We expect people to understand us from our behaviours. I believe the boss should know from the employees' actions whether they are loyal to the company or not, and doing the job right or not, without the employees visiting their boss trying to prove themselves with words, sentences, paragraphs or stories. I rarely verbalise my feelings and thoughts. But after experience, I feel I am being unfair to myself. Speaking out and putting my thoughts in clear words is the way to understand and be understood correctly. I now make an effort not to rely only on my actions, because I really care not to be misunderstood.

CASE BLOG 5.7

John: Run, tackle, run, tackle

I think definitely "actions speak louder than words" – although, in a lot of circumstances, words are required, because seeing the actions does take time. I used to play a lot of football. The captain would say we all must "run, tackle, run, tackle" – it used to kind of go in one ear and out the other. Once on the field you would forget it. But when you saw the captain himself "run and tackle and run and tackle," the actions were very persuasive – his actions made you very motivated and pushed you to do the same thing. In this instance, his words meant little, but his actions were very motivating. I suppose what I am trying to say is that words are required in certain circumstances, whereas in other circumstances words mean very little – it is the actions that count. Someone can tell you to trust them, but until they behave towards you in a trustworthy manner, you are unlikely to trust them.

CASE BLOG 5.8

Mariyah: A note to parents

Another example I just thought of is one that is far from the workplace – parents. They say parents have to practice what they preach, and in many cases, they just preach and don't practice. Here, the child doesn't always turn out according to what they told him because he saw no real example (action) to follow. But if they preached less and practiced more, it is more likely the child would have become the way they wanted him or expected him to be. In this respect, communication through a role model is imperative to provide numerous and relevant cultural cues for learning to take place. It is the Do's and Don't's in a culturally-acceptable situation when people communicate!

BLOG VIGNETTE 5.5   Sorry, Sorry, and Sorry

How many times do we say "sorry" in our daily life and at work? How many times do we say sorry when we did something wrong or think we did something awkward or unpleasant? How many times do we feel sorry but do not say so out loud? Interestingly, my favourite section of the *Gulf News* (www.readers@gulfnews.com, February 19, 2010) discussed the issue based on the poll results taken from hundreds of readers. The question was "When is 'sorry' considered essential?" and "When is 'sorry' considered merely a masquerade of behaviour?" The result of the poll (Q: I always apologize when I upset someone) indicated that 81% say sorry when they know and realize that they have done something upsetting, while 19% *did not*. Too few people indeed! Yet, the majority of us still seemed to say sorry consistently – verbally and written. In fact, I have realized that saying "sorry" is almost embedded in my daily speech, to the extent that I find it difficult *not* to say it, especially if I experience any kind of dissonance in my mind and feelings. Does this mean that I am not apologizing out of sincerity and regrets, but rather out of habit? As one person in the *Gulf News* column said, "Apologizing has become a habit rather than a sincere expression of regret." Wow … that is a deep and complex statement. How do you react to that poll result when in certain cultures, people are trained to generously utter the word "sorry" as not to offend someone, maintain a harmonious situation, respect the person you are interacting with, or as simple as out of politeness? In the United States, where I spent years of my education, I was confronted with a situation where a friend of mine irritatingly replied to my apologetic words with, "Hey … you don't have to say sorry!" Over the time, out of habitual practices, I didn't or couldn't stop. Likewise, Dania, a Jordanian student of mine, says she apologizes regularly, yet stresses that these apologies require a true intention. Khaled, who is from Lebanon, describes an apology as a noble, yet necessary, act – often requiring actions beyond words.

CULTURAL LESSON 5.5: THE HIGHS AND LOWS OF APOLOGIES

From a cultural perspective, people are shown to apologize for many reasons. Studies have shown that in Asian culture, for example, people are more apologetic. They use the word "sorry" more often; for example, they might begin to say "I am sorry that..." when they want to deliver bad news. The person would utter such a line because they know that the news will hurt the receiver. It is also common for a person to apologize when he or she knows that the word "sorry" will soften the other's heart. In this sense, apologizing is used as a weapon or strategy for more effective communication. In essence, "sorry" is used to communicate one's sincerity, humbleness, regrets and politeness. Asian people would normally use such a strategy and manner because they are part of a high-context culture which prioritizes and values relationships over task orientation.

According to Ting-Toomey (1999), the face-saving concept is another explanation for why Asians use an apologetic form of communication to maintain relationships. It is expected that if someone realizes something will disrupt a harmonious situation, his or her immediate reaction is to offer an apology. Hence, saying sorry is of the utmost importance. But, sometimes in Asian culture, people do not say "sorry" because people are expected to understand that the word is implied with nonverbal cues, for example, showing an apologetic face or taking immediate actions to remedy the mistakes made. This raises the question: Can silent language indicate a more sincere apology than a verbal or written apology?

On the contrary, in another culture, such as a low-context society, saying "sorry" is not required as frequently as in a high-context society. Job tasks are to be conducted based on given objectives, purposes and reasons. If things do not happen as planned, then that is okay. There is nothing to apologize or feel sorry about. Even if one feels sorry about it, it is not necessarily to be uttered over and over again. In a low-context culture, you must express regret in a concise and succinct manner please! Say it only when you mean it!

CASE BLOG 5.9

Dania: Habit of apologizing

I agree that the habit of apologizing to others by saying "sorry" is strongly connected to culture, whereas a person that comes from a culture that puts relationship first tends to use that word a lot and tries to always express their apologetic feelings. Unfortunately, I am such a person. I say "unfortunately," because people tend to take it for granted. I believe that we have to express our "sorry" if there really was a mistake from our side, and not just keep on using it for whatever reason just to escape from a situation. This is because people will reach a point where they do not see the apology as true! I also think that if a person is the task-oriented type, the word "sorry" will not mean as much; rather they will prefer to just fix what went wrong.

CASE BLOG 5.10

Jaber: Cultural influence

People are influenced deeply by their own culture, in terms of their behaviours and responses. Saying sorry is worth a lot when you are from a culture that makes relationships a priority, but it is worthless in societies that think about business and personal benefits first. Due to today's global situation, we are no longer different nations without any communication or interaction. Each nation's culture is influenced by the cultures of other nations, which modify contextual meanings of saying sorry to one another. Sometimes it is difficult to say sorry to the person, even if you know that you are wrong and you have to apologize. This might be due to personal beliefs or behaviours, or due to the counter party's way of understanding the true meaning of an apology. Many people take an apology as the remedy to all problems. They tend to apologize only in order to satisfy their managers, or to close the case and continue with their life.

CASE BLOG 5.11

Mathialagi: The many faces of sorry

In India, very often we say, "Westerners have departed from India and while going they left us two words – 'thank you' and 'sorry.'" People say sorry for various reasons, like when they feel guilty, because of habit, artificial apologies and sometimes just to close the discussion if they want to avoid the conversation. People say sorry when they feel they have hurt someone and this is one way to tenderly apologize. It is very crucial how this is communicated and who is communicating. If the person asking for forgiveness keeps repeating mistakes and repeats this word, then he loses credibility. "Sorry" is also seen as one step to patch up differences, and a matter of courage and dignity. It depends on who says sorry, to whom, reasons for saying sorry, and the forum to say it.

CASE BLOG 5.12

Khaled: The importance of an apology

For sure, I will say sorry whenever I feel that I may have misbehaved, hurt someone or done something wrong that another person didn't like or felt angry, sad or uncomfortable with. Saying sorry will not make you appear lower in front of the other person. However, it will make you gain a better relationship with the other person, where he will appreciate your kindness and politeness, and the way that you handle the situation, along with the speed of your reaction. However, saying sorry in some cases will not be enough, as from my understanding, in many cases, I think an action should be performed as well to correct the situation, as per the kind of relationship you have with the person. For example, as for me, I will correct a situation with my friend by saying sorry, along with a hug maybe or a pat on his shoulder, even looking in his/her eyes. This way, I am offering a message to the other person that I am really sorry and am offering a sincere expression of regret.

BLOG VIGNETTE 5.6 No Matter What, I Will and Shall Not Brag!

It is weird to think that, years ago, I could never say "I am great at..." or "I have achieved..." On many occasions where I could have mentioned my achievements or knowledge, I kept my mouth shut or pretended not to know anything, essentially playing dumb. This is because in my Malaysian home culture, it is not acceptable to brag about oneself. Let me illustrate my culture through the behaviour of my six-year-old niece. One weekend, she had a wonderful time vacationing at a theme park at Makassar, Indonesia. The next Monday at school, she spread out her theme park map on her desk. She then started to say to herself, "Been there, been there, been there," speaking in a low voice, barely audible to anyone more than one or two meters away. Soon, her friends began to gather around and ask her, "Hey Irdina, where did you go?" Then she modestly and shyly said, "Oh, oh, I went to Makassar last weekend." Within minutes, many questions came pouring in, investigating all the details of her vacation. With this opportunity, she excitedly told them everything – once they *asked* her. My twin sister and I had a good laugh when we analyzed her daughter's subtle behaviour. Both of us agreed that we were very proud of her for being modest. She didn't want to brag about her vacation, unless and until she was asked. She did so indirectly by invoking the curiosity of others about what she had done. As we reflected, she could easily just have announced the trip to her friends by saying, "I went to a huge theme park last weekend and enjoyed it tremendously!" We thought she was well trained culturally because as anticipated, she didn't or perhaps couldn't?

CULTURAL LESSON 5.6: BRAGGING? IS IT THE WAY OF COMMUNICATING OUR ACHIEVEMENTS?

According to Webster's dictionary, bragging is when someone constantly tells people about something at which they have succeeded. So, if someone exaggerates or talks excessively about his or her shining success, that counts as bragging. It is true in all cultures that people who talk excessively about their glowing success are deemed to be braggers. Every human who listens to over-the-top self-aggrandizement will agree that it is bragging.

Such behaviour also reflects the bragger's personality; that is, a person who likes to show off can be considered boastful and arrogant. But what I would like to discuss now is the proper degree of verbalising or communicating one's success. How does one decide whether to discuss it? If bragging is considered an excessive promotion of oneself, then in my culture, even a minimal use of words such as "I am good at…" can be judged as boastful. It has come to such an extent that in Asian high-context culture, people are less willing to say anything positive about themselves, especially using the words "I did something great…"

Typically, in the Asian culture, we are trained to be modest and humble in our speech and actions. No achievements or successes should be announced by oneself at any price, particularly using the word "I." Others should do that *for* us. Others should recognize what we did or what we have accomplished. Recognition, compliments and accomplishments should be awarded by others; the concept of collectivism – of "we" – can be applied here.

On the other hand, in an individualistic culture, people are used to saying things about oneself. It is an acceptable and common practice for one to state one's own achievements. I used to feel so strange when I would hear my Western teammates say, "I can do this and I can do that" with such confidence, whereas I, who had the same qualifications, could not even begin to verbalise my accomplishments, let alone write a glorious statement praising myself. But over time, I have mastered the skill of communicating my expertise with both confidence *and* modesty. We can actually balance those two aspects, I have found, and I am less hesitant about the decision to articulate my achievements.

So, now that making a decision on verbalising my achievements is no longer a problem, the challenge is not *what* to say, but rather *to whom* I can say it with pride and joy, *when* a situation really warrants me standing up tall and stating my achievements, and *how* to say it so that I sound humble, modest and not arrogant. These decisions are definitely up to each individual, but their source is our cultural roots, that is, how we were taught by our society to state our achievements. Like my niece, whose mummy preached to her to always be humble and not boast about her life. She then learned that she could still share her accomplishments, but in a very indirect way. The end result was that she still managed to catch the attention of her friends.

When we think about communicating our accomplishments, culture affects us on two levels: our personal decisions on how to communicate, and organizational decisions involving many people in a group. As a global manager or employee, one needs to be sensitive to both levels. Understanding the cultural roots of your colleagues requires you to deeply explore thoughts, feelings and actions. So, next time, when one of your colleagues or employees blushes or becomes speechless about his or her own accomplishments, quickly pat his or her back. Or, if he or she is unable to say an accomplishment out loud, dig it out of them and trace the performance so that you can offer the appropriate compliment.

On the opposite side of the coin, if one of your employees or colleagues announces his or her success, take it as a form of demonstrating dignity and pride, rather than boasting. Whether the person is shy, boastful or justifiably proud of his or her accomplishments, decisions about rewarding performance are to be made. Do not judge someone at work based on cultural ignorance, but based on awareness and sensitivity of their cultural roots – and your own. As an Australian, my student John expectedly stressed the necessity of citing your own achievements in the workplace. His blog entry, however, shows a rich understanding that other cultures may not agree. I suspect this awareness will make him an excellent manager in a multinational firm. Similarly, Farah, who is from Lebanon, takes a practical approach to communicating her achievements, overcoming her cultural tradition to promote career success. Nasser is yet another example of a student of mine from Dubai who does his best to be modest, yet uses bragging when it is strategic.

CASE BLOG 5.13

John: Business lingo

When it comes to the business world, it is a difficult call on when and how to state your achievements. I fully appreciate that some cultures do not feel comfortable speaking about themselves, or that some personalities are shy and reserved. But in the business world, in many instances, there just isn't the time for these cultural nuances to always be understood and catered to. In a fast-paced environment, managers need staff who do speak up, who do sell themselves. Unfortunately, this could often mean that some people will be left behind, often the people who are better at their jobs. International managers need to call upon their cultural awareness to realize that many people need to be pushed and prodded to talk about themselves. This awareness will help them to recognize the best people for their efforts, rather than for coming from a culture that encourages them to speak up.

CASE BLOG 5.14

Farah: There is a time for everything

I come from a culture where bragging about one's self and achievements is not welcome at all, and I personally do not admire much people who bluntly brag just to fulfil their egos. I think we should differentiate here between bragging about achievements and speaking up when there is a need to speak up. At work, for example when you are in a situation where you have to show your knowledge and defend your case, then definitely go for it – this is not bragging … and you should get all the support from your manager. When you are being interviewed for a job, you have to shine, you have to modestly state your achievements – otherwise you will lose your chance! I support modesty in actions, proving one's knowledge at the right time, in the right situation, and with the right audience. It is better to prove your knowledge through your actions, rather than saying "I did..." or "I achieved..."

CASE BLOG 5.15

Nasser: Apply bragging when necessary

I believe that the situation and environment call for either the use of bragging or modesty. For example, sometimes there is a need to show off your achievements, especially if you know that if you do not show off, you will lose. I am from the UAE, and in our culture modesty is a good thing, but sometimes it puts you in the shade. If you don't talk about your accomplishments, you will be forgotten. In work situations, managers and people at the top form opinions about an employee according to things they know about them. So, if they don't know your achievements, then it is as if you are not achieving. My idea about bragging is, use it only when you need it. Don't talk about your achievements in front of people who have fewer accomplishment than you. Rather, talk about it in front of people who are higher or equal to you in achievements. I believe bragging can be good or bad, depending on the timing and the people.

CULTURAL REFLECTION 5.1: YEAH, CULTURAL UPBRINGING DOES SHAPES YOUR COMMUNICATION

The way people communicate reflects their cultural upbringing. In the Asian culture, from a young age, we were taught on what, why and how to speak to different people. However, for Westerners, context doesn't really play a role; instead, content is considered critical. Reflect on your own culture and answer the following questions:

- Why do people speak the way they do?
- How does context matter when people communicate with different cultures?
- In what ways do people use indirect communication styles or direct communication styles?
- What are the factors that influence the way people speak?
- What is the influence of culture in determining which styles to use when communicating?
- Do people consider nonverbal cues or verbal cues important to develop an effective message? If yes, in what ways do these different cues matter in cross-cultural communication?

CULTURAL REFLECTION 5.2: A PROMISE IS A PROMISE!

For anyone, an ideal picture would be "A promise is a promise." In business, deals are sealed through contracts where once you sign, it means you will honour your written words. Is that the case in all cultures? Several situations play out differently in a different context and in a different culture. The issue is: Can a promise be broken and reworded by altering a business contract?

- Describe a situation where you faced someone who did not fulfil or keep his or her promise. Then, explain your reaction. Were you understanding, angry or frustrated?
- Why do you think this person demonstrated the behaviour illustrated above? Why do you think you reacted as you described? Use relevant cultural dimensions to briefly analyze the situation and behaviours.
- On what basis do people make promises? Discuss this based on the concepts of individualist and collectivist cultures.

CULTURAL REFLECTION 5.3: CONTEXT OR CONTENT?

Are you dependent on context or content when you aim to communicate with someone? Do you apply verbal or nonverbal cues to emphasize the meaning of your message?

- Imagine a situation where you are faced with a problem. How do you recognize whether people are being honest to you or hiding their thoughts and feelings about something important?
- What are the different communication patterns observed in the workplace based on different cultures?
- Why are communication styles using a verbal manner preferred by one culture, while nonverbal cues are preferred in other cultures?
- In which situation would you consider silent language a powerful way to communicate your behaviours? How about using direct messages to deliver your thoughts and emotions?
- How do you perceive space and time when communicating your message? Do these two factors influence the way you communicate? Can you provide a scenario in which space plays an important role? In which situation is time essential when sending a message?

CULTURAL REFLECTION 5.4: SAY SORRY, WHEN, WHY, AND HOW?

Some people believe that "To feel sorry is one thing, to say sorry is another thing and to actually mean it – is immeasurable!" Reflect on a situation where you have used this word to express your feelings to others. How do you communicate it?

- In your daily life and at work, when do you find yourself saying sorry, and to whom?
- Is it all right to say sorry over and over again, even if one does not mean it?
- Does saying sorry need to be backed by further actions?
- Why do you say sorry? How do you say it?
- How do these behaviours connect with your own culture?

- Have you noticed differences in other cultures around you?
- What kind of issues arise around apologies within your workplace?

CULTURAL REFLECTION 5.5: BRAGGING: WHY AND WHEN DO WE DO IT?

In trying to make sense of the way we communicate, we must reflect on our communication styles, patterns and approaches. Let's revisit a key concept called "bragging" as one approach of communication and analyse our patterns of communication and practices of communication.

- What is the meaning of "bragging?" Provide definition and support it with examples, incidents or situations in which you encountered someone who bragged in your eyes.
- Why is "bragging" considered an accepted norm and behaviour in your culture? In what situations is such behaviour not acceptable as an expression of thoughts, feelings and actions?
- Do you communicate and share your accomplishments in the workplace readily in front of your colleagues? How about to your family members? Close friends?
- How do you communicate your successes or failures to your friends, family and colleagues?
- Why do different people communicate their success stories in an exaggerated manner, while some do not like to disclose them?
- What are the factors that explain the act of disclosure about accomplishment or sharing of experience and/or information with others?

5.1 @CULTURAL PONDERS

Actions Speaks Louder Than Words, So It Seems!

Malak Al Aamiri
Autumn 2010

I do think that actions speak louder than words. And you don't even need sometimes to know the person in order to understand what he means when he makes a certain expression. I face it daily at work, I do it and everybody does it. Yesterday, we were at a brainstorming [session] with our chairman in order to find a creative idea and turn it into a profitable project. We were six people around the table. He started explaining the idea and elaborated for about an hour, trying to tell us the point that he was trying to explain. Once he was done, he looked at us, seeking responses. He didn't say, "Now it is your turn." We just understood that he was done and started to respond. From my side, I told him what I thought, and he was shaking his head like saying, "Good, you got it," which encouraged me to speak even more and elaborate on the subject. Once I reached the end, he started to look to the others. I knew that I had started right, but now I was going wrong; he wanted someone to interrupt me and correct me, while he couldn't. So I looked to my colleague, and he proceeded with his thinking until we reached an agreement about the overall idea. The bottom line is that we don't need to speak at all. It's very hard for women though. Did you even wonder why we have two eyes, two ears, but only one mouth? It means we need to see, hear and then, if necessary, talk. Or if you don't understand what you hear or see, we can talk. We have a saying: "If the words are worth silver, then the silence is worth gold," which is stressing that silence is sometimes worth more than saying words or commenting on something. We are living in a big world, with many people in different families, in different countries, different cultures, in different contexts, and it does make sense that we will be different in our communication styles and the way we send messages to each other.

5.2 @CULTURAL PONDERS

Listen, Could You Please Say It Nicely and Politely?

Amr Jamal

Autumn 2010

In my opinion, all cultures ultimately follow the same manners and are trying to drive and lead people to behave in good ways. All cultures actually give us the guidelines that they think are right and acceptable to follow. For example, there is *no* culture that promotes stealing, killing, cursing or swearing ... just in some cultures, the emphasis on manners is stricter and stronger than in others. For instance, in some cultures, to be polite and behave with good manners is more important, and other cultures are more relaxed about those manners. For example, if you want to ask someone to do something for you, you know it's better to say please. In my office, my manager, he's from Pakistan, when he is asking me to do a certain job, he is just ordering me. That's not because he doesn't know he has to say please, but he is from a high power distance culture, which makes him think if he is the boss he can say or ask whatever from me without me questioning him. But my previous manager would ask, adding "please" at the end of the sentence because he was from a low power distance culture. So I can't tell my manager, "Now mind your language, I'm not your slave, I'm an employee," because that's what he has learned from his culture. But in the end, as John mentioned, I'm happy that I'm more educated and more culturally sensitive than him.

6

Cross-Cultural Negotiations

It's a well-known proposition that you know who's going to win a negotiation; it's he who pauses the longest.

Robert Court

BLOG VIGNETTE 6.1   Negotiation – It Is an
Outcome! Really, Isn't It a Process?

That evening, in order to set the tone for the weekly theme, I threw a basic question to the class: What do you understand from the concept called negotiation? With confidence, Pradeep briefly said, "When two parties reach an agreement on a subject matter!"

Suresh instantly probed him: "How about an instance when there is a conflict? Or what about when the two parties cannot agree on one single aspect? What if there are alternatives to a decision to be made?"

Impatiently, Christina put up her hand, and said, "Let's consider one step behind. Let's look at negotiation as a process where people express their ideas and then discuss and deliberate, provide alternatives, and then opt for the best way to reach an agreement."

Suresh said, "I don't and can't agree! From my experience, I observed negotiation as '…beginning only when or if a conflict of interest arises, or else it would only be defined as a decision-making where you will arrive at a consensus!' Negotiation takes place when two parties in a room fail to get their objectives agreed upon!" He gave a reassuring look to the class.

Although Marisa was nodding throughout the class, she was also confused. With courage she said, "Can I clarify? I sense that there are two views on the concept of negotiation. On one hand, I agree with Pradeep and Christina. They define it as a process where people obtain an agreement after going through several phases before they reach an agreement. On the other hand, I think Suresh's argument also made sense. He is more interested in the outcome of a conflict because to him, negotiation only transpires when two parties cannot reach a decision."

At that point, I could sense that the class began to understand this conclusive rationale: whenever individuals do not agree on the points or the agenda brought forward in a discussion of any sort of work matter or business deal, then "negotiation" begins.

If things are in agreement or acceptable, then there is no need for a negotiation process. After 30 minutes of discussion, I intervened by saying, "I am happy that we managed to critically dissect this meaning. But, what about cross-cultural negotiation? How different is it from the meaning of negotiation that we just brainstormed?" The rest of the class looked enthusiastic to begin another round of discussion. Roberta voluntarily said, "The difference lies not in the outcome or the process, it is in the human dynamics – the people who are involved, because they are the ones who stir the process or the outcome to a direction. They bring their culture to the table!"

Suddenly the class was quiet and Christina enthusiastically said, "Now we begin to explore this concept deeper!" and I saw everyone nod in agreement.

I teased them by concluding, "Are we not negotiating a definition now?"

CULTURAL LESSON 6.1: SO, WHAT IS CROSS-CULTURAL NEGOTIATION?

According to our class discussion as illustrated above, the concept of negotiation is defined as "beginning only when or if a conflict of interest arises." If things are in agreement or acceptable, then there is no need for a negotiation process. I am happy that we managed to critically dissect this meaning.

Negotiation, according to the standard dictionary definition, is "a process of bargaining preceding an agreement." Does this mean that bargaining implies a conflict of interest? Or does it mean that people bargain when they want a better deal? Yes, it is true people normally bargain for betterment. For example, people make counteroffers to what has been offered in order to reach concessions. And that, in essence, is a disagreement, right? Not agreeing to the terms set, not agreeing to the time frame, not agreeing to the people involved or not agreeing to perform requested tasks at all in the first place. Many layers of potential disagreement exist.

One thing for certain is that, if we are to be engaged in cross-cultural negotiation, then we need to understand the art or skill of bargaining based on different cultural values. For bargaining itself has a different meaning in different cultures. If this is the case, then disagreement needs to be understood across cultures, so that a blunder can be avoided and not created. Blunders, in turn, can lead to more disagreements, consequently leading to undesirable business deals or working environments.

In the field of cross-cultural management, negotiation practices have been discussed as culturally rooted behaviours. Without doubt, one's personality can contribute to different practices. But, one's negotiation style can also be attributed to the shared practices of one's national culture. Take a look at the cultural dimensions that we have learned, the concept of power distance, for example. In environments with high power distance, there is a strong line between those who are able to negotiate authoritatively and those who are unable or not allowed to express their disagreement.

The opposite is true in low power distance cultures, where disagreements can be expressed without barriers. Negotiation behaviours are also contingent upon people's communication styles. Low-context people might find it easier to state their disagreements in a concise and clear manner, whilst high-context people may bargain and voice their disagreements using body language or silence, or via a mediator or an electronic medium such as email. Some of my students believe that one's negotiation style is determined by one's character or personality, while I argue that negotiation style is very much determined by one's cultural values. My argument is backed by a wide range of research that confirms negotiation styles are culturally rooted.

CASE BLOG 6.1

Khaseefah: Negotiation is an art!

Negotiation is an art. My perception of negotiation, from my own experience, has shown that negotiating can be an art that one can nurture and learn throughout time. Indeed, given my reserved personality, I learned throughout my student and very recent working lives that resolving conflicts of interest is delicate and requires an art of communicating arguments wisely, if not tactfully. However, this communication skill cannot work without having strong insight into the other disputant's culture, as this is an advantage in anticipating the reactions of the person, and eventually the outcome of the meeting. As Dr. Norhayati stresses, "negotiation style is also much determined by one's cultural values," which suggests that an understanding of culture and awareness of negotiation styles can guide us to determine strategies for presenting the issues and solving them. To me, the whole process of negotiation is based on the approach presented to the disputant, and the ability of this approach to convince and solve the matter, all related to a thorough understanding of the cultural values and negotiating styles of the other disputant. This is picked up from a series of personal or professional experiences, whereby we all learn from mistakes, observations and others' behaviours. Therefore, the broader our cultural understanding, the greater our ability to get the other side to comply with our demands. Of course, it is not always this simple, but the cultural awareness, values and negotiating styles which vary from one country to another are definitely guidelines to bear in mind to help us shape our own communication styles, as well as to shape our own personalities. Thus, cultural awareness is a useful tool in life to conduct negotiation processes optimally.

CASE BLOG 6.2

Eliyah: Negotiation is a culturally rooted skill

I recognize that negotiation is not a competitive activity, but rather that, unless the parties collaborate to reach agreement, even short-term solutions may fall apart. Negotiation is a skill which is culturally rooted, which we can improve during our lives. For people who are more flexible and collectivist, negotiation is real bargaining and a cross-boundary activity. In addition, there are multiple approaches to negotiation, for example problem solving, compromising or forcing. With the problem-solving approach, participants openly exchange information about goals and priorities and actively search for alternatives to meet both parties' decision criteria. On the other hand, by employing the forcing approach, one party can use the position they have to force other parties to agree with them. In my opinion, negotiation using the force approach is more common in some cultures, such as those heavy on individualism. Also, some nationalities are more negotiable compared to others. This means the factor of nationality has a more significant effect on negotiation compared to other layers such as religion, age, education and organization.

CASE BLOG 6.3

Kamila: Win-win, win-lose, lose-lose, lose-win

I disagree with the following statement presented in class: "Negotiation begins only when or if a conflict of interest arises." People do negotiate when conflicts of interest arise, but that's not the only reason for negotiating. I like what our colleague Khaseefah said: "Negotiation is an art that needs to be crafted and designed to suit the negotiation table that we are sitting at." I believe that this is a very important point because we normally negotiate in different places such as work and home. The way we negotiate at home is totally different from how we negotiate in the workplace; that's why negotiation must be shaped appropriately to meet its various objectives. Negotiation ends up with four different situations: win-win, win-lose, lose-lose and lose-win. I normally negotiate with my brother at home when we would like to decide on something or solve a problem, and we usually end up with a win-win situation.

CASE BLOG 6.4

Rafeeqah: Negotiation is not a one-man show

Negotiation is not a one-man show. It is a skill that varies from one person to another and is shaped to a great extent by the culture of the negotiator. Not everybody has this skill, especially considering that to be a good negotiator you need to have good communication skills, that is, be a good speaker. I cannot tell how diplomatic a negotiator should be, or should learn to be. I suppose it depends on who is at the other end of the negotiating table.

It happens weekly, if not daily, in our lives, when we sit for discussions with our line managers, subordinates or colleagues. Most of the time, there is at least one negotiator around the table who is unhappy or critical about the way the negotiation is going. Is it cultural differences that cause this distress? I don't think it is always because of culture.

You know what we all should worry about: What really scares me is how two negotiating parties can have totally different comprehensions of the concept of "negotiation." It happened four years ago with me, when I was called by my line manager with all my team members to negotiate the implementation of a new curriculum. Our manager, I understand (just from taking this course), was from the power-distance family. She believed she was always right and didn't admit if any of our ideas were good. She refused to listen to any of the members' suggestions. I gave an idea and tried to explain it. She was really upset and accused me of interrupting her. I answered back on the spot and in front of all the members (I still don't know how I behaved that way, as this was not my typical personality, nor my Arabic culture). She didn't accept that and we proceeded into a lengthy debate.

To negotiate means to change our minds, to find the truth in the words of others, and to try to convince or become convinced. What makes a negotiation fail, however, are negotiators with deaf ears, like my manager – they hear you but do not listen. In this case, there is no way to reach an agreement. Wish you all the best of luck, hopefully with managers who are good listeners, and thus good negotiators!

CASE BLOG 6.5

Anastasia: Negotiation is a mutual agreement

I support the concept given by Dr. Norhayati and shared by my colleague that "Negotiation is an art that needs to be crafted and designed to suit the negotiation table that we are sitting at," and indeed, I believe it is better and more useful to "understand the cultural background of the opposite negotiating person or party." I also agree with my colleague Miss Rumaisa that "Negotiation is something we do every day" (even if it is bargaining a very simple issue) at home with families, spouses and kids; in the market; at work with colleagues, subordinates and superiors. I would say negotiation is progressively built in each of our characters since we are born; it could be enhanced and it varies with exposure, education, experience and friction, and, of course, it depends on personality and type of character.

Why do some of us are born with "negotiation skills"? And how? I would say a newly born child is a good negotiator, because he knows how to attract his mother's attention by crying for milk, and sometimes just crying to be held – and he gets what he wants most of the time. When this reaction becomes abusive, the doctors advise his mother to start ignoring him until he refrains from excessive crying and gradually refrains from this habit. Hence negotiation and bargaining is part of human nature. It is sometimes more professionally exercised and now studied, but you still can see an uneducated trader in the bazaar (in my country of Ukraine) making a very good living with his strong negotiating and bargaining skills, acquired purely by experience. In my country, bargaining in the market is something very normal and an essential part of the culture, which gives each of us early acquired (primitive) negotiation skills. In this case, however, I wouldn't call it negotiation, rather dictatorship or a one-sided instruction or order. I believe that for a negotiation to take place, you would need a mutual agreement of both parties to discuss and reach a certain settlement on a certain idea or deal.

BLOG VIGNETTE 6.2   Who Is at the Other End of the Negotiation Table?

We often negotiate at our workplace – either in a formal or informal manner. On one hand, when it comes to a formal style, managers will normally prepare in advance strategies and tactics to face the negotiation. Such strategies are to facilitate and ensure that the process is successful. On the other hand, the informal manner takes place when you have a conversation with your friend, you suggest one thing, and then she countersuggests another thing. For example, you might suggest going Starbucks for a coffee. Your colleague disagrees, and says, "Let us try a café called Arabica; it is new in town and I heard it has different taste since it has imported coffee beans from many different countries and has a Japanese owner!" The communication and process of negotiating takes place spontaneously wherein both parties are debating which café to go without any prior formulated strategy to win the other over to the decision to be made. Returning to the dictionary definition of negotiation as "the process of bargaining that precedes an agreement." In essence, we communicate, we argue, we debate, we propose, we deliberate, we agree and we disagree. In going through the process, however, we often encounter many frustrations and complexities due to differences in behaviours and personalities. If a manager faces challenges with varied individual behaviours, the negotiation process can be further intensified when the manager deals with people from different cultures. The key provoking question is thus: who steers the negotiation table and who has the upper-hand in doing so will drive the negotiation process to a winning outcome!

CULTURAL LESSON 6.2: HAGGLING AS A TACTIC OF BARGAINING

Consequently, cultural issues will impact the outcomes and decisions reached through negotiation. So, if we look back at the definition of negotiation – the "process of bargaining preceding agreement" – then I can further provoke the question of how do culture influence negotiation process? In some cultures, perhaps the concept of "bargaining" does not exist (particularly in a formal context), for example, in a high power distance society where we may not have the luxury to bargain in the first place. In such a respect, we ask, "Can we bargain fully if that requires us to voice our true opinions and say things out loud?" On the other hand, bargaining and exchanging ideas are common practices before coming to a decision or agreement in certain cultures, whilst in certain cultures, bargaining may not be allowed during the process of negotiation!

Consider another situation – a very informal one – the marketplace. We see in high-context societies, such as China, Malaysia and Arab countries, that haggling is a common practice. People bargain and bargain over prices and quantities until both parties are fully satisfied. Additionally, we also observe people carrying this attitude over to a formal business setting, for example, continuing to bargain even after the contract has been signed! This always seems to frustrate other parties if they are from a low-context society, as they are used to concrete deals with fixed and predetermined price-tag. Thus, I ask again and question the dictionary definition: Do we bargain before a decision is made or do we still bargain after the decision has been made? This all depends on the culture in which we engage in the negotiation! An interesting concept to keep in mind as we all negotiate in our daily lives, both formally and informally.

I remember when I was negotiating with colleagues at my university in Malaysia about getting an assignment I wanted. I was trying to be very straightforward about my choice, putting my request down on the table, stating what I wanted and how I wanted to do it. This was the "straightforward" communication style I had developed through my long training in the United States. I thought it would be much easier for everyone for me to approach the subject forthrightly, rather than keeping silent. I did not want to be pushed around in terms of what I could do and what I was uncomfortable doing. To my dismay, this negotiation style did not go over well with my high-context colleagues. They thought I was being overly aggressive and selfish by verbalizing what I wanted. I was only allowed to send a proposal to my head of department explaining what I could do. Once my superior made the decision, then he would discuss the result with me, that is, give me my assignment. I was perplexed and frustrated, as I had hoped my superior would hear me out and listen to my requests – I believed the end result was negotiable. It was then that I learned that when you are dealing with people in a society of high power distance, negotiation takes another perspective. The question of *who* is at the other end of the table is significant, as authority assigns negotiators hierarchical roles within an organization.

CASE BLOG 6.6

Rayyan: You never get a second chance to make a first impression

It is true, we always do bargain and negotiate in our daily lives, either formally or informally. It is hard to debate about when we should usually negotiate, after a decision has been made or before that! In my opinion, it depends not just on people's cultures but the situation they are involved in for bargaining and negotiation. From a cultural perspective, if we are dealing with people from a low-context society, such as Westerners, it is usually difficult or even impossible to bargain after the decision and contract have been made! This American proverb clearly defines this situation: "You never get a second chance to make a first impression," meaning that when dealing with people from a low-context culture, you should be straightforward and bargain before any decisions have been made to agree on both parties' interests. You cannot bargain after the decisions have been made.

However, this might be different in certain situations. Here is a scenario: Imagine you are doing business with a Western company. This is not the first time you have conducted business, and there is a trust bond between you. You know their interests and they know yours; you have come up with a psychological contract and mutual adjustments among yourselves. In this situation, you can easily bargain because there is a long-term friendship between two parties. As a conclusion, we need to evaluate with whom we are bargaining and the situation, as well as the culture. Then, accordingly, we can adjust our behaviour.

CASE BLOG 6.7

Bahayah: Power distance

As I understand negotiation, it is give and take, receive and send, until we get to an end that will satisfy us all. When I got my current job, I negotiated with the contract manager about my job title and about the amount of salary, knowing the amount had already been set, but still, I did attempt to negotiate. In fact, and as my colleagues mentioned above, high-context cultures, such as in my home country of Bahrain, always negotiate! I learned from my dad first and from work experience that I should take as much time as needed to get to the agreement point that will satisfy me and the other party. It also depends on the employee or manager's reaction during the negotiation. Their reaction gives you a clue if it will end soon or last for many more hours! This is the thing I hate the most about negotiation. It takes too long to convince the other party and then make the deal or forget about it.

Power distance is one of the limitations in negotiation. Last year, my manager sent me to lead the quality team to convince another department quality team that cooperation between our departments would be a first step to improvements internally and externally. When we entered the meeting room, unexpectedly, the first thing the manager said was, "Who has the highest position of you? Who is the one going to talk to me?" I found this shocking and embarrassing, even though I was excited to be the one in this position. From that time, I understood this manager had a harsh style of communicating with people at work. So, I convinced myself that, whatever he said, I would not let his words hurt me. I smiled and calmly explained to him that I was the one who was going to speak and I started introducing my group to him. And then we went through the subject in detail. I succeeded in obtaining his acceptance, and the deal is still going on until now, although I try my best to keep a distance between me and him by always giving the details of our discussion to my manager, so they can deal with each other on their own power level.

CASE BLOG 6.8

Sahiqa: Negotiating with Arabs

Arabs are known in the marketplace for negotiating until they have reached their satisfaction, as if they strive for a 100% discount. Strangely, however, they tend to back off from negotiating in the more formal work environment, and many lack the confidence of being vocal in terms of expression towards their boss. Here in Dubai, the boss is the boss and he does what he thinks he should do. Why should he have that position if people are to argue against his orders?

I still think that the manager should be the manager, that he should keep the role of making the orders, and that we should accept these orders with respect. At the same time, the manager should be open to any upcoming opinions or ideas, which can lead to improved results, or learning something that hasn't triggered in his mind yet. I think communication between colleagues and maintaining good relationships with managers is very important. In the end, it's all about being understandable, that's all.

CASE BLOG 6.9

Taiif: Who you are dealing with is crucial

I completely agree with Shahiqa; she is 100% correct about the negotiation skills of Arabs when buying stuff. However, as she added, when it comes to work negotiation, things change. There are many different cultures here in the UAE, where you need to adapt yourself to the style and culture of the person on the other side of the table. What I mean to say is, if I was in my country of Egypt, I would know how to deal with the person negotiating with me, as I know we share the same culture. On top of that, the person I would be negotiating with would also not be affected by other people from different cultures, as they would be in the UAE, which leads to some differences in the way he is speaking to you and negotiating with you. We need to know the person on the other side of the table very well, as small details in negotiating may spoil the entire negotiation and lead us to a dead end or perhaps not getting what we really wanted.

CASE BLOG 6.10

Jamal: The diplomatic way

I agree with Gabriel, that saying "no" is much better than saying "yes" and then never achieving what had been requested. For me, I do not use "no" as word, maybe because of my culture or my childhood growing up in Jordan. Rather, I express my refusal in a diplomatic way. If it happens that my boss asks me to do something that I am unable or refuse to do, I will express him my refusal in the same moment, by using my facial expressions first (with a hesitation look), and then slowly inform him, and try to convince him (if needed) why I will not able to do it. I think I can identify myself as being somewhere between high- and low-context culture. From the low-context side, I appreciate people who encourage others to express their feelings without any shyness. For me, I try to make sure that the person of whom I am making a request is really sure of his decision; I insist by asking him to let me know from the beginning whether he can or cannot. Although this way does not work with everybody and in every case, it is one step towards making people around me (at work and home, and with friends) feel more comfortable.

One more point. The previous subject of relationship-oriented vs. task-oriented cultures has a lot to do with saying no to our boss. If employees have good relationship with their boss, they will be more comfortable in expressing their feelings, even if they are from a high-context culture.

CASE BLOG 6.11

Maeena: Saying "no" can be easy, yet difficult

I think saying "no" to the boss can be both easy or difficult in different situations, depending on the relationship between the boss and employee, the size and culture of the company, as well as the cultures and personalities of different employees. For example, in my culture, it is not very acceptable to say "no" to the boss, and usually people should obey their manager. But I'm a different type of person who always disagrees with my boss if I don't like his ideas or solutions and think certain tasks can be performed in a better way! And surprisingly, I can see my colleagues are all silent when the boss establishes new rules or structures and nobody likes it – nobody says a word. Still, I don't know actually if it is good to disagree with the orders, because in some cases it has created many arguments, and the boss refuses to accept his mistake ... and only in a few cases have I convinced the boss that he is mistaken!

CASE BLOG 6.12

Raavi: It is always a tricky situation

Saying "no" to the boss is always a tricky situation. You always feel cornered when you receive requests from top management, as you believe there is no way to get around doing them unless you have a valid reason. In our Indian culture, saying "no" would be considered very rude. We find it hard to express a negative response verbally or nonverbally. We usually express ourselves in a way the other person wants to hear, and it should be done delicately. It is always good to know your boss from inside out. Maintaining a good relationship with your manager is always a plus. Also, sometimes we need to pay attention to how he handles situations, so that by understanding him well you come to a point where it is not hard to approach and negotiate with him.

CASE BLOG 6.13

Saeedah: Zero tolerance

I also agree with Galagher and Jabeer that saying no in the first place is better than not being able to perform the task later on, but in addition to that, "no" should be said in the right way and at the right time. It is correct that some cultures have zero tolerance for the word "no" being said clearly and boldly. In such cases, it is better to use phrases such as "I'm not sure I have enough time..." or "Another suggestion could be..." Such techniques are very useful with superiors who usually stick to their ideas and are not very open minded in terms of wanting to change. I work in a finance department, and in finance, it's much better to say "no" in the first place and not complete the job than to do it wrong, because significant actions could be taken, leaving room for large mistakes.

BLOG VIGNETTE 6.3   Pad Thai Negotiation Day: Please Give Us Extra Shrimp

I was having lunch with my best friend that week in a Thai restaurant where we are regulars. As usual, we ordered Pad Thai, a dish of stir-fried rice noodles with eggs, fish sauce and shrimp – a famous dish on any Thai menu. When the waiter came to us, he greeted us with his usual smile. We were lucky that day because we did not have to wait for a table outside, as there were no other customers (it was only 11:30 a.m., after all). He asked us if we wanted the "normal dish," implying the Pad Thai we always ordered, and we said "yes." Then my girlfriend, who is from Tunisia, told him,

> Give us more shrimps, last time there were only a few. Come on, we are your regular customers. Please add three or four more.

The waiter, who is from Thailand, was blushing at that moment and modestly said,

> "I can't because that is the rule, only three shrimps for Pad Thai."
> I was already laughing by this time. My girlfriend persisted. "Come on, please, please give us more shrimps."

The waiter nodded and left. Then, after 10 minutes, the dish came and we ate our Pad Thai with much delight, until my girlfriend noticed, "They didn't add the shrimps!"

We called the poor waiter, and my girlfriend asked him again, "Hey you did not give us the extra shrimps, come on, we are your regulars, we come here every two days!" Her tone of voice was joking and both she and I were laughing.

"I am not the chef, I am not cooking, I can't do it," said the waiter.

"Just go to the kitchen and just take the extra shrimps," said my friend.

CULTURAL LESSON 6.3: YEAH, IT IS THE ASIAN WAY OF NEGOTIATION!

That incident got me thinking about negotiation styles. I am perplexed and amazed at the way my friend was willing to negotiate her shrimps. I had read that Arabs normally use emotional appeals when they negotiate, as well as the haggling technique, with the key characteristics of persistence, patience and insistence. My friend did try her luck three times, demonstrating patience to wait for the waiter's responses in order to understand why she did not receive the extra shrimp. My friend also used the relationship-based appeal by saying "We are your regular customers," although that was only our fourth visit. We had, however, developed a rapport with that particular waiter (that is why he asked if we wanted our "normal" order). On the other hand, the other negotiator, the waiter, used an entirely different strategy from my friend. He first politely stated his reasoning by objecting to her request.

However, after an unsuccessful effort of convincing us, he simply smiled and obligingly nodded in agreement. Believe me, I nearly thought that my friend's persuasive smiles and pleas had succeeded. Finally, when he was questioned for the final outcome, only then did he provide an explanation for not offering us extra shrimp ("I am not the cook!"). So, he had used nonverbal cues (smiling), followed by politeness, and the last resort of pointing the finger at someone else, as if saying, "I am not accountable for your shrimp count." I still laugh out loud when I think of this incident.

The mismatch in the negotiation styles of the negotiators was clearly evident. On the one hand, my friend was really persistent and thought the strategy of pleading (as one of my students said "using the salesperson/marketing style") would be a winner. On the other hand, the waiter was using what he thought would be a winning strategy, which is politely explaining the situation, then nodding and smiling after the negotiator's demand without any confrontation. Hence, both represented opposite directions of negotiation – avoidance vs. confrontation. At least my friend took the situation lightly, although I know she was frustrated by not getting her extra shrimps. The waiter too escaped from fulfilling the request made by my friend, as he failed to please his customers.

Consider the same scenario, but with different people. What if another person had used an even more aggressive communication style than my friend? Or a more passive one? Can a difference in negotiation style lead to a better decision or outcome? Or was our shrimp shortage simply due to us dealing with the wrong person, that is, a waiter who had no authority to make decisions? Had it been the manager who greeted us, perhaps my dear girlfriend and I would have enjoyed our Pad Thai with extra shrimps. Bon appétit! Until we see more of each other … perhaps at a Thai restaurant with better luck, and a winning negotiation skill.

CASE BLOG 6.14

Jamila: A decision-maker and a satisfactory agreement

A successful negotiation should happen between individuals and groups of individuals who are decision-makers and capable of reaching a satisfactory agreement. The Pad Thai incident above was not a successful negotiation partly because of two elements: Firstly, the item being negotiated was a standard dish served to everyone with a fixed quantity and price, and, secondly, the waiter was not a decision-maker, which led to a failure in the negotiation process. As I mentioned above, a successful negotiation needs to involve someone who is empowered to make a decision.

CASE BLOG 6.15

Bahiyah: You are not in a position, are you?

I agree with Jamila that perhaps the negotiation was not successful because the waiter was not in the position of making/taking any decisions, whereas if your friend had been negotiating with the manager of the restaurant, he/she might have considered the customer loyalty factor (as your friend said, "We are your regular customers!") and relented to your request. Surely, the cost of two more shrimps would be much less than the cost of losing two loyal customers.

At one point, you thought that your friend had succeeded in the negotiation due to the waiter's different cultural background. His physical response of nodding was taken as agreement, whereas this was only a polite way of saying no, or perhaps stalling or buying time, so your friend would not walk out before the order was served. Only when you had finished your lunch did the waiter verbally communicate his incapacity to fulfil the demand. So, his way of negotiating was mostly indirect and physical, while your friend's way was very direct and verbal.

CASE BLOG 6.16

Jasha: A mutual understanding

Successful negotiation depends on so many things, such as mutual understanding, decision-making power, agreements on the points by both parties, favourable conditions for doing any negotiation, the will to negotiate, and relationships between negotiators. In the restaurant case, I agree with the comments that the waiter obviously did not have the power, and the company's policy did not allow him, to give extra shrimps. He was not the person to make such a decision. Also, he might not have had close, friendly relations with the chef.

CASE BLOG 6.17

Lateefa: Perhaps use diplomatic and professional style

The problem in this negotiation was that the friend misunderstood which players in the restaurant could make decisions. In Arab society, a person can negotiate with the buyer or service provider and reach the desired outcome. As an Arab person, the friend felt that she developed a relationship with the waiter because she had been a customer for some time, which, to her, meant that by now the waiter should know her in a way that she could ask for more shrimp. On the other hand, the waiter's response to her explains the restaurant culture and the formal rules and regulations for making the decision not to offer extra shrimps. I think she needs to change the way she negotiates and try to recommend or comment about the quality of the food to the manager, in order to encourage cooperation and to receive extra shrimp on her next visit, I hope without paying extra money.

CASE BLOG 6.18

Eiliyah: The process of bargaining

In my opinion, when negotiating we should consider the meaning of negotiation, which is: "The process of bargaining with one or more parties to arrive at a solution that is acceptable to all." This means that if we are sure our negotiation will not have any solution, then it is not actually a negotiation, but rather a discussion. In this case, we know the waiter doesn't have any authority about this issue, and thus there is no solution, so perhaps this is more of a discussion than a negotiation. In this case, the waiter doesn't have a role to make decisions, as he mentioned to the customer. This makes the interaction an unsuccessful discussion. Also, national culture is one important aspect we should be aware of. For example, if a case such as this happened in my country of Egypt, after two requests for more shrimp, the waiter would be angry and he would treat his customers badly. But here, in Dubai, I believe that customer satisfaction is a very important factor and the culture of being "customer orientated" is very sophisticated, especially in restaurants, hospitals and hotels. Because of this culture, the waiter was patient and, instead of getting angry, just explained he was not the decision-maker.

CASE BLOG 6.19

Muna: The final decision-maker

Not all negotiators have the right to make decisions. They negotiate and try to come up with some scenarios to be agreed upon or refused by their boss, who is "the final decision-maker." The example that Dr. Yati shared with us shows how employees' empowerment adds up within a business and keeps customers satisfied and loyal. It is obvious that the waiter isn't authorized to take decisions, even if it is only to add some shrimps. I think negotiation with those who don't have a say or can't make a decision is just a waste of time. I made this mistake once. I worked at one time with a supervisor who listened to our complaints, negotiated solutions and gave promises, yet implemented nothing. We found out later that things were not under his control and it was the superior boss's decision. We live in a world of hierarchy, I guess. Now, I try to make sure to complain to the person in charge who can really solve the problem by actions and not only words, or else I prefer not to complain and "just let it go."

CULTURAL REFLECTION 6.1: NEGOTIATE HARD, BARGAIN TO THE BONE

Let's refer to the above phrase that teaches us about the art of negotiation across cultures. Reflect and analyze some of the key questions when you are preparing for an effective cross-cultural negotiation process. You need to consider the following aspects:

- *Preparation*: How much control do you have over the negotiation setting? Where would you meet your client – home turf of either party or a neutral environment? How would you adjust to the unfamiliar environment, that is, when you experience jet-lag effects?

- *Relationship building*: How important is the relationship with the counterpartner in steering the negotiation? Would engaging in prior interactions facilitate the expected outcome of the deal?

- *Exchange of task-related information*: What types of information should be made available or communicated to the counterpartner during the negotiation? How transparent do you need to be to ensure clear agreement on the deals to be closed? How quickly do you need to deliver the information needed?

- *Persuasion*: What are the strategies or tactics you would employ? Do you think making a direct request or stating clearly what you want is a strategic move? What do you think about keeping silent before or after the offer? Which strategy proves to be a winning strategy? Why? Explain based on cultural dynamics and reasoning.

- *Concessions and agreement*: How do you arrive at an agreement? Verbal or written? Are contracts signed between two parties considered binding for both parties? Can you make changes?

CULTURAL REFLECTION 6.2: YOU NEED TO ESTABLISH A RAPPORT!

Anatolia Mehmet, the marketing manager in a reputable firm in Istanbul, has finished her meeting that day in the office and is overwhelmingly exhausted. Unfortunately, she will have another dinner meeting later that evening. Her mind is too tired for another meeting. But she needs to prepare and be alert, as the meeting will be with a Chinese team who wants to present their products and its costing. It will be an instrumental meeting to establish a new network of suppliers. Nonetheless, Anatolia is very anxious. She knows nothing about Chinese culture and has never done business with them before, but they are offering good opportunities. As far back as she can remember, her colleagues have told how arduous the process is dealing with the Chinese since they are reserved and aren't normally keen to express their feelings. Worse, they might not be able to make decisions impromptu unless their senior management is in the meeting. As a Turkish woman from a strong culture of hospitality, Anatolia enjoys warm trust and connecting with others during their first encounter.

Thus, many perplexing questions run through her mind. As a consultant who can guide her, here is a series of questions for Anatolia to prepare for the dinner meeting in just a few hours' time.

- What kinds of preparations should she make to win the negotiations?
- What kinds of "warm-up" conversations should she begin with?
- How can she establish a good rapport in a short time during dinner?
- What can she expect from this team during the negotiation process?
- If she were to close the deal, could the team respond with immediate answers? Does she need to bring a colleague of the same rank/position with the team of the Chinese suppliers?
- Should she pay for dinner as a courtesy and hospitality since the Chinese businesspeople visited Istanbul? Would such behaviour signal a good relationship to be established between them? Or should she let them pay if they insist?

6.1 @CULTURAL PONDERS

Cross-Cultural Negotiation? Personality + Culture Bound?

Ahoud Yusof

Autumn 2010

To be a good negotiator, one must be good in articulating her or his arguments, and must have convincing points. All of the people today view their own ideas as right and the best, but how do we convince others? Again, I think that is part of someone's personality; it relies insignificantly on one's culture. Some people are happy to negotiate and reach a point of agreement, while others put their feet down to clearly emphasize their ideas as right. Despite such an approach being considered unprofessional, many people can't help as it it's part of their nature. Consequently, it is what people believe in. Obviously, there is little you can change in a habit of a person unless they are willing to do so. So, I realized that when I am in an argument, the best solution and thing to do is to present your points in a calm way! Try to achieve a win-win situation. Usually when people are being stubborn, fighting for themselves with their voices above each other's heads ... what does that do?! For me, it gets you nowhere! Whether or not it is in life or in a workplace, one should understand that they have to be diplomatic. And in order to grow and succeed in negotiation, a person should listen, accept and respect because the outcomes we are looking for are not conflict but reaching an agreement! Something people don't seem to understand is you must live life with its simplest form and you don't have to be perfect because no one is complete. Eventually, everyone likes to be appreciated and respected. I mean so what if your point of view or idea was proven wrong? It's like you have to be wrong at times in order to learn and make a better decision one day! So, my conclusive point based on this discussion about cross-cultural negotiations and skill development: people have formulated their characters and personality. My question is thus; How do one's personality and cultural values fit in when negotiation takes place? This is truly a crucial question to answer.

7

Cross-Cultural Decision-Making

Sometimes success isn't about making the right decision, it's more about making some decision.

Robin S. Sharma

BLOG VIGNETTE 7.1   Strange, You Don't Make Your Own Decision?

I remember my professor in the United States once asked me, "Why did you come to the States to study?" I proudly announced that my father was happy to see me study in the United States, as my two other siblings had also studied there. I thought that was the most ideal answer, but it was also my honest answer. To my dismay, she threw back this question with shock in her eyes: "So your father made a decision to where and which college you go to?" I nodded with a nervous smile and said, "Yes." My argument to my professor at that time was, "We are different in our cultural orientations. In my culture, decisions are happily tossed around the people we are close to – to the extent that we don't even mind our mother or father paving the road for us!" In my culture, decisions are made interdependently and collectively. The outcome of a decision is shared among the "in-group" who contributed to the process. In my case, I sat down with my father, my mother and my siblings. We discussed, we deliberated and we listened to each other. Finally, when my father suggested I study in the United States, I took this as my final decision. I was willing to follow what he suggested without hesitation. After all, I did not see the decision as being only about my life; rather, it was about "We, us and ourselves." My parents meant a lot to me and going to a college was a fundamental part of my life. Undeniably, I needed their blessing for the choice I made. But this does not mean they forced me into it.

CULTURAL LESSON 7.1: INDIVIDUALISM VS. COLLECTIVISM IN DECISION-MAKING

From a cultural standpoint, decisions can be made in two different ways. The first kind of decision-making is interdependent and collective, which rests on an affective and risk-averse orientation. For example, in my Asian culture, decisions are made based on the authority of a boss, and often subordinates will defer to authority to determine what kinds of decisions they can make or when they can make them. You should not make a decision in light of oneself unless you are told to do so by a higher-ranking superior, such as a boss. Also, decisions can be based on the tightness of a relationship with family or close friends, known as an "in-group." Thus, in a family setting, a father carries the same authority and power as a boss in the workplace – with the final say. On the other hand, people who are considered part of your "out-group" comprise strangers or acquaintances, people with loose relationship ties. In this particular culture, the boundary between in-group and out-group is crucial for decision-making, because it allows you to decide to what extent information should or should not be disclosed and shared, to whom you want to deliver such information, when such information is disclosed and how to best disclose it.

A second mode of cultural decision-making is one where decisions can be made independently, and people prefer a linear process of thinking to arrive at a choice. My professor is an example of an independent decision-maker. Returning to our conversation about university selection, at the end, she said the following:

> When I went to college decades ago, it was my sole decision. Once I made the decision, I only announced it to my parents. From childhood, we were taught to be independent and think of what was best for our own selves, and our own lives. I believe that one needs to think on their own and not be influenced by anyone because it is their own life.

With that exchange, we both smiled at how our different cultures influence our decisions. In an individualistic culture, decision-making is an independent process where each person has the autonomy to decide what is best for "I, me, and myself." Other people can contribute to that process by providing information to support the decision, but others should not and cannot significantly influence your mind, feelings and actions to arrive at the final result. Decisions rest in the hands of the individual, and he or she is accountable and responsible for the results. Generally, in Western culture, people will employ a sequential, logical and rational method to first weigh the pros and cons of a decision.

For example, in the United States, people will identify the issues first, then gather all the facts, think of possible alternatives or plans, and then weigh each of the plans carefully before arriving at a decision. It is a step-by-step sequence, and each of the steps is an independent thinking process. For instance, in team decision-making, each individual can provide inputs at each stage of the process. One is empowered to think on their own two feet wherein information exchanges and sharing are expected to facilitate the way the team makes decisions. One's beliefs and values take precedence over others and may not have ultimate repercussions on how the outcome of the decisions takes place. It is an independent thinking process.

This is in strong contrast to business cultures of countries such as Japan, where decisions are made based on a consensus process, in which discussions take place at multiple layers and management structures until the entire team is satisfied and in agreement. In Japan, decisions are made contingent upon an interdependent process, either through a hierarchical structure or collective effort.

CASE BLOG 7.1

Farah: Fact vs. intuition

Farah, who is from Malaysia, generates a powerful observation about communicating and making decisions with an American team members during her experience working in a global virtual team project. Farah shared her experience of working with a team member who is from Austin, Texas, in the United States. We use very few words, and in most of our conversations, he speaks in a way that is straight to the point; decisions are based on fact rather than intuition. Most of our discussions end with actions. We rarely talk about personal problems. In the way he sends personal messages to me, it is clear he strives to use precise words and intends to be taken literally.

CASE BLOG 7.2

Abdoulla: Accepting risk

For Abdoulla, who has worked in banking and real estate for a number of years, the only thing certain in decision-making is being uncertain. Every decision involves a certain amount of risk. If there is no uncertainty, you do not have a decision; you have a set of steps or a recipe that is followed to bring about a fixed result. Linking that to culture can also have a great impact on decision-making. People who are risk takers with low uncertainty avoidance will tend to make decisions faster than those who have high uncertainty avoidance.

CASE BLOG 7.3

Pauline: Respect for elders is key

Hailing from a high-context society, it is part of our culture to make decisions based on the advice of our elders. At the workplace as well, we make our decisions with the final advice of our peers and managers. The final outcome and the influence our decisions have on people around us are therefore very important to us.

CASE BLOG 7.4

Leu: The context is clear

Leu presents an acute observation of a high-context communication style employed by one of her teammates in the team project. I would like to take the example of one of my teammates who uses a high-context communication style when negotiating. He is from Colombia. He applied a face-saving approach and often is more likely to ask for assistance than to work out a solution independently. He always uses words such as "I can..., if...," "Yes," "I agree" and "Okay" to agree with our group decisions after all of us have expressed our opinions and come up with a solution. But I realized that my experience in global virtual teams provided me a good insight about the different communication styles. Over a few weeks, I learned about low-context communication styles and I find myself trying to shift my own communication style to a low-context one in order to make everything I say clear and understandable, yet it is challenging.

BLOG VIGNETTE 7.2 An Asian Way of Making Decisions

Believe me, even the decision-making process has its own *rules of the game* contingent upon one's cultural context. Several years ago, as I was lunching with my research collaborator, Prof. Suki Hiroshi at Kyoto University, we discussed the complexity of making decisions and the concept of the "rules of the game." As he asserts, there are no formal prescriptions, such as company policies, statutes, constitutions or court decisions.

Instead, the rules of the game are the unwritten rules, attitudes and expectations to which one must pay attention. They are more complex and deeper than what is stated or written. Hence, when decisions are to be made, members must observe attentively who makes the decision. Alas, Prof. Suki said, with an intense voice, the most important criteria are *how* decisions are made! As an Asian, I could relate to his rules of the game concept. I laughed and jokingly said, "For me, it's easy: listen and follow what the boss wants – and then get him to decide! In my culture, making decisions has its own protocol and process. One cannot override the process. Nor can one ignore the protocol."

He laughed and said, "What? You also accept protocol as the basic element of decision-making? Between you and me, our cultures are in sync. You see, I believe in following rules and adhering to protocol, because that is exactly what and how the Japanese make decisions. Every inch of the process has its own contextual rules and principles that no one should ignore, but abide by." At the end of the discussion, both of us arrived at a consensus that complexities in the decision-making process begin with knowing the rules of the game through keen observation and meticulous consideration of the dos and don'ts. That process elucidates what culture is all about.

CULTURAL LESSONS 7.2: THE POWER OF RELATIONSHIP AND CONNECTION

In Japan, there are distinctive cultural practices based on two specific, unique management principles known as *wa* and *amae* rooted in Japanese cultural values. Japanese society represents three basic cultural values – harmony, peace and tranquillity – essentially, the concept of *wa*. Furthermore, according to Deresky (2008), for Asian cultures like Japan, decision-making patterns are based on patience and cooperation, consensus decisions and participative management. People generally do not use a confrontational approach when conflict arises. Instead, they use a diplomatic, polite way of indicating or expressing disagreements using nonverbal gestures. This strategy is based on an important Japanese principal called *wa*, signifying peace and harmony. The principal of *wa* is rooted and manifested in the cultural value called *amae*, which means indulgent love that emphasises physical and spiritual harmony. The key concept can be examined in management practices such as decision-making, conflict management and the negotiation process (Deresky, 2008).

Japan is known for its unique culture, yet its intricate value system can be challenging for other cultures and Western society to understand, appreciate and acculturate to accordingly. Unlike Eastern culture, Western culture promotes a different decision-making strategy when dealing with conflicts and disagreement. People use confrontational strategies that allow dialogues among the involved parties until the matters or problems are solved. According to Hall (1976, 1990), high-context people focus on relationship building with their collaborator. They need to know the individual and read and interpret different communication cues. Therefore, high-context and low-context people develop different computer-mediated communication message styles. For example, high-context people may use nonverbal symbols to articulate relational cues. Some common cue substitutions are icons and electronic paralanguage, for example, emoticons and parenthetical messages like caps, boldface and italics in emails. High-context people might also say things indirectly or subtly, or present implicit messages to set the appropriate tone in collaboration efforts, another aspect of nonverbal communication behaviour. High-context people may appear more courteous due to their polite and apologetic words to maintain a harmonious relationship.

BLOG VIGNETTE 7.3   Come on, Make a Decision!

In last week's class, we talked about making decisions. We also divided into two teams to play a short game, which involved each team deciding what to bring if they were to become stranded on an island. Each team of four or five players was told it could bring only three items, and that it had three minutes to make a team decision. I'm not sure whether that would be possible in real life – four or five different minds making a crucial life and death decision in such a short time frame! I closely watched the different dynamics of the two teams. Indeed, interesting! One team was calmer than the other, as well as less talkative. The talkative team, on the other hand, seemed to be engaged in more negotiation and deliberation. By the time the minutes ticked away and the time was up, the talkative team had failed to make a decision, while the other had resorted to a quick team decision. Not surprisingly, both patterns emerged in our two class teams. So, whatever it takes for you to make a decision depends not only on your cultural values, but also on your individual ability to decide. Team members may share similar cultural values, yet the members may have different personalities that can result in different approaches to decision-making. For example, someone might procrastinate in making a decision because of the above constraints. Or, could there be a situation in which someone is eager to make a decision but is constrained by an authority, that is, due to a situation of power distance?

CULTURAL LESSON 7.3: THE CONSTRAINTS OF DECISION-MAKING

Decisions – why is it that these are so inevitable in our work and life, yet always so difficult to make? Based on the business dictionary, the definition of a "decision" is "a choice made between alternative courses of action in a situation of uncertainty." This means that decision-making presents people with many choices based on a range of alternatives, and that actions are dependent on one's preferences. The lesson from the class exercise I mentioned in my blog was that it is very difficult to make decisions under certain conditions, including:

- Time constraints: Some people seemed to want to discuss the issues at length, and were not concerned about the limit of three minutes. Imagine if a bomb was about to blow up!
- Information constraints: Not knowing the situation well enough, that is, where the island actually is and what is available on the island. This information would have helped the teams decide what to bring.
- Group dynamics: Different thoughts, emotions and actions. Some team members seemed to communicate and others remained silent. Some became very expressive and emotional about their impending deaths on the island, and others were angry that their ideas were not accepted.

Not only do these constraints themselves matter, but cultural dimensions can help explain the reactions to the constraints. For example, a culture may adopt either a monochronic or polychronic outlook, meaning different views of time, and thus respond to decision timelines and deadlines differently. Information constraints can also influence how people analyze a situation. Some people, for example, will use factual data, while others will turn to emotions, such as my students in the game who were more focused on dying on the island than the tools they needed to bring. Some people will prefer to make decisions by working in a team, while others will make decisions based on individual needs. Either way, one must make a decision!

CASE BLOG 7.5

Rada: Business decisions

The class decision-making exercise stirred up some strong responses from participants. As Rada demonstrates, frustration felt by the students was similar to what many had felt at work. In business, facts should rule and help us decide. It is very important to look up facts and study the implications of all possible decisions before we select the best. This is because your decision will cost you or your organization. Sometimes managers decide not to decide and ignore the time factor. This might be out of fear of the implications, especially when they are aware that others will be affected by their decision. This is why managers should communicate with their employees to better understand their ideas and concerns and hence to get familiar with facts that help them make better decisions that are in favour of all.

CASE BLOG 7.6

Salim: Team effort

Salim shares his formula for making effective team decisions at work. It is based on his personal experience in making decisions at work, which I have simplified into the following stages:

- Trying to know the exact required action from management so that I can focus on achieving the same.
- Trying to get all the required information from the team.
- Involving my team in the decision-making process by holding brainstorming sessions so that we can come to the most appropriate decision with the most benefit to the company.
- My rule in decision-making is that two heads are always better than one.

CASE BLOG 7.7

Shania: Be considerate

Shania takes a collectivist interpretation of our class exercise. When making a decision, it is very important to consider not only yourself but the people affected, especially in a work environment. I really believe that all of us need to work as a team. It is very important to share ideas even if there are conflicts. I do agree with the argument that if you work alone you will contribute more to your individual project than a team project. Yet, there are so many situations in life where other people must be part of the decision-making process. Such situations can seem impossible to solve, as conflicts will remain dominant due to our different decision-making and thinking styles. So, what is the best solution? In my opinion, it is to reach to a point that satisfies all parties, similar to the bargaining process, wherein one person offers to pay 130 for an item, while the seller asks for 140, and then they settle on 135. So, to reach that point of agreement, one must give up something to gain something. In the above situation, what was important was for each party to understand that they were not standing alone and thus had to compromise.

BLOG VIGNETTE 7.4 A Struggle between Relationships and Power Distance When Making Decisions

How does a relationship link to one's status in the workplace? Is it possible for a relationship to overwrite the formal authority one has, or the other way around, for a relationship to suppress one's authority? Is there such a thing as a "power-relationship struggle when making decisions"? Let's contemplate such a situation through the lens of my expatriate friend Nina and her boss Anuksha based on her own descriptive narrations.

That morning, Nina wanted to see her boss, Anuksha but was faced with a resistance. A week before that, she had discussed some documentation and had set an appointment with her boss for a 5 p.m. meeting to quickly run through it again. But by midday, on the day of the appointment, Nina had some meetings cancelled. She thus called the secretary to ask if she could come in earlier because she was free at that time and preferred not to wait until the evening. Nina excitedly informed her secretary that the meeting would only take 10 to 15 minutes.

The secretary told her:

"Hold on, talk to her, she is here!"
With enthusiasm, Nina said, "Hi Anuksha, can I see you for just 10 minutes or so?"
Her response was simply, "Hi Nina, let me look at my calendar first, and I will get back to you quickly."

Nina waited for 10 minutes, then the secretary called her and said, "She can't meet you because she is occupied right now and she said since she is meeting with you at 5 p.m., just wait 'til then." Then her secretary further asked Nina,

> "Is it okay, Nina? or do you still need to see her earlier?"
> Nina eagerly asked, "Can I request for anytime earlier than 5 p.m.?"
> The secretary checked and then replied, "No."
> Nina said with a frustrated tone, "Then let's wait for 5 p.m., then."

The situation ended with an abrupt response without room for negotiation. The thing is, Nina has known Anuksha for several years now and have developed a good relationship with her – at least from her own standpoint. Alas, to Nina, Anuksha is not a stranger to her, nor do she considers their relationship to be what one defines it as "an arm's length relationship." For example, on a personal level, Anuksha has invited Nina to her home for dinner and have shared details of their personal lives. On a work level, they have collaborated on a few projects in the past. However, over the years, from a professional point of view, Anuksha climbed the ladder into a management role and became Nina's boss. Due to her strong leadership accomplishments, Nina, was, and will always be very happy for her. Yet after that day's encounter, Nina was dumbfounded. Her puzzlement was not due to the fact she was unable to squeeze in a time to meet her, even for 10 minutes. Nina could totally understand that her boss was occupied and Nina had, after all, secured an appointment for later in the day. But the incident did strike her for a number of reasons.

What made her upset, first of all, was that Anuksha hadn't picked up the phone and relayed the message to her, as she had promised, "I will get back to you quickly." Secondly, why did she need to go through the secretary, an intermediary, when they have an established relationship? Since Anuksha looked at her calendar and knew a meeting was not possible, naturally, she could have gotten back to Nina instantly by giving her a call. Why did she need to waste her time by calling her secretary to announce the decision to me, as Nina questioned the situation in a bewilderment tone. With a frustrated voice, she went on to say:

> "Instead, Anuksha could have used the time she took to refer to her secretary by directly calling me in just a flash.
> Why did such a simple task require such a hierarchical process?"

CULTURAL LESSON 7.4: POWER DISTANCE IS ACCEPTED AND TOLERATED

Let me analyze Nina's situation above based on key cultural dimensions. In his theory, Hofstede (1984) explained that power is perceived differently in the workplace in different cultures. He integrated power with the concept of distance, which describes the level of acceptance of inequality in workplace. In essence, this dimension illustrates how, on the one hand, people in some cultures see power as a hierarchical concept, with large gaps and the expectation of inequality, for instance, between top management and lower management or between a boss and subordinate. On the other hand, other cultures observe power with individuals on more of an equal standing, with low or no barriers between top and lower management. Overall, power distance tells us to what extent power is distributed based on organizational structure.

Anuksha's situation made me think about this concept of hierarchy in the decision-making process. She is a boss, hence the significance of power distance. Her behaviour is totally acceptable in a culture of high power distance, where a message is delivered through another person, that is, her secretary. Hierarchical cultures are process driven, with many layers. Anuksha, after all, comes from India, where hierarchical power relations are common. Perhaps the problem in this story is Nina, who failed to understand this reality simply because she tends not to favour a hierarchical structure, with the belief that it slows processes down. Perhaps this is a situation fuelled by a dilemma between relationships and power.

According to Hofstede, the dimension of collectivism explains the need for relationships between people, and why and with whom people establish relationships. In the workplace, people usually create bonds in order to achieve a harmonious environment and sense of belonging with an in-group. An in-group is considered a group of people with whom you have strong social ties, such as family members, spouses, close friends or colleagues. A member of an out-group is a person with whom one has established an "arm's-length relationship," or a stranger with whom one has no connection of any sort.

In a collectivist society, such as in my home of Malaysia or Anuksha's home of India, once a relationship is developed at work, there is an expectation that the relationship will help one get their job done in a harmonious manner. On the contrary, in a high power distance culture as prescribed by Anuksha, she is merely exercising her power and authority to steer her subordinate into a hierarchical system. Thus, relationship takes a back seat, and status comes into light. It is not a question of right or wrong about Anuksha's behaviors as manifested in the above illustrated situation. Rather, the answer is how do we make sense of her culturally-rooted behavior from the lens of collectivism vs. power distance. In essence, Nina is seeking for a relationship based solution, whilst Anuksha is demonstrating a high power distance status. For example, when one is considered a friend, her or his request should be honoured and respected. Conversely, in an individualistic culture, such as in the West, whatever decisions are made at the workplace will be based on task-oriented goals, with relationships coming secondary.

This aspect also reminds me of Trompenaars and Hampden-Turner's (1997) dimension of specific vs. diffuse, which illustrates the distinction between personal and private boundaries in the workplace. Hence, the boundary between the in-group and out-group also results in the development of separate private and public spaces, as Trompenaars and Hampden suggested.

When a person considers themselves a member of your in-group, then that person feels that your relationship formed at the workplace will override formal authority or power held. You are expected to do favours for this person based on the personal relationship. However, in a specific-oriented society, the culture clearly outlines that friendship is not or should not be allowed to intervene with the boundary of professionalism. Work is work, play is play, and these aspects should not be intertwined. The motto is: "You are my friend, but in the workplace you are my colleague or my subordinate, and those two boundaries should not be crossed."

In the light of the situation between Anuksha and Nina, the relationship they had established seemed to be inconsistent with the power distance principle. From the point of view of Asian cultures, which are based on collectivism and where relationships are a priority, one would anticipate that there would be an overlapping boundary between the private and public space (also based on the diffuse dimension). As such, an expected behaviour would be for Anuksha to say to Nina, "Sure, come over, we will chat for 10 minutes (due to their long-standing friendship)."

However, since Anuksha subscribes to the high power distance of Indian culture, her action of asking her secretary to call Nina was indeed a lesson of power and authority at hand. Therefore, looking at these two key dimensions in an Asian culture, it became apparent to me that somehow it is incongruent to the cultural values embedded in one's expectations. Strong formation of relationships breeds into diffusion of boundaries – personal and private. One is expected to build a relationship, yet one is also expected to respect the power the boss holds – even if the boss happens to be a long-term best buddy.

So, when you have a historical relationship with your boss, how should you react when she or he plays a hierarchical power dynamic with you? Do you or can you say to her or him, "Are we not friends?" or "Do you not like me?" In the above illustrated case, if I could deduce, perhaps Nina could say to Anuksha, as a friend, "Why can't you pick up the phone and let me know whether you can meet me?" However, as a subordinate, Nina should accept that Anuksha's secretary will and should call her!

Indeed, this is the cultural dilemma in the decision-making process: How do you balance personal relationships and task-oriented ones when the power distance is one we are likely to stumble into in the global workplace? Blunders such as this happen, leaving us to make sense of them. When the realities and perspectives of how situations should be handled by two or more different parties are mismatched, frustration seeps in, along with misunderstanding and misinterpretation. Additionally, behaviours of those from other cultures inform you of the thoughts and emotions they have for you, for they are manifestations of their perceptions. You then begin to question the perspectives of others by considering the meaning of their actions which, to you, seem foreign.

For me, I question the way and means Anuksha communicated to her friend Nina. Evidently, from her perspective, she is a friend, not a superior, to her. Nina seemed to give the significance of the friendly relationship to her primacy over thinking in terms of the discourse of power. In the end, Nina contradicted her own cultural background of high power distance. Yet, personally, for me, I like my relationships to come first, and I do not want power differentials within them.

A key question is: How is it possible to achieve this camaraderie in a culture that values high power distance? Yet there is another way to look at this situation, and likely the way Anuksha or Nina would explain this story. Theoretically, the concept of power distance allows you to understand in what form a relationship exists and the boundaries one should have within that relationship. It tells you that if you acknowledge another person to be your boss, then you should respect the relationship to that extent. In a hierarchical culture, you accept that inequality takes place and that the relationship should not be abused based on friendship.

BLOG VIGNETTE 7.5   Are You a Stranger? Can I Trust You?

As children, our parents often remind us, "Don't talk to strangers!" Why were you taught at a young age that it is not permissible to talk to a stranger? Why is that you are reminded again and again that talking to a stranger will lead to something harmful because they are strangers? Is there an underlying reason to identity the roots of cultural values in terms of recognizing the boundary of privacy? In a culture like mine, we were educated about not *being friendly* to strangers. Instead, only speak to the in-group, that is, people like family members and friends. With them, we would be comfortable to exchange our secrets, so to speak, because we trust them. For out-groups, we were taught to be cautious in terms of our privacy boundary which indicates the level and reasons for trusting others.

It is easy to identify someone as a stranger when you can see that person face to face, because then you will notice that person is not someone that you are familiar with nor do you recognize. But what about in virtual space? For example, in a global virtual team context, most of the time you are collaborating with someone without the history of working together and fewer opportunities to meet face to face, assembled with culturally diverse team members only for temporal basis projects. Likewise, someone can be a stranger, yet also be part of your "friends" network on Facebook – perhaps because they are a friend of your friend's cousin's daughter – which can lead to multiple layers of "knowing strangers."

Why would you befriend that person? Can you trust him or her? It makes you think of the advice given by your parents years back and you start to ponder: "How do I decide? Can I or should I trust or not trust this person?" What are the culturally rooted values that affect whether "To tell or not to tell?" in the case of working of together at a distance? How do you choose whether to disclose between private vs. public information sharing?

CULTURAL LESSON 7.5: RECOGNIZING TRUST AND THE BOUNDARY OF PRIVACY IN GLOBAL VIRTUAL TEAMS

The key lesson to learn about cultural difference is: How do people define the truth and trust concepts that are embedded in one's beliefs and cultural values as well as manifested in one's rule of privacy-rooted behaviours? As Trompenaars and Hampden-Turner (1997) clearly asserted, the decision "To tell or not to tell" primarily depends on the specificity of the condition or situation faced at work. They introduced two key dimensions of the boundary people put between work and personal: diffuse vs. specific. In diffuse cultures, people expect work and personal agendas to be integrated, thus making it difficult to differentiate between one's own and another person's goal.

So, in such a culture, people see work and personal lives as interlinked and interconnected by an established relationship with the in-group members, such that it is a challenge to express the truth in order to maintain trust. For example, in the American culture, what one desires to disclose depends largely on the instrumental value of it. The reason for information disclosure is not based significantly on the relationship, but more of a purpose or utilitarian goal. In another culture, people can easily draw the line between what can be disclosed and to what extent you want to disclose without jeopardizing the relationship.

In the teamwork environment, trust is most crucial because you need to work with people with whom you may not have any historical background. This is especially true for global virtual teams, where people are assembled or assigned to fresh sets of teams located in different parts of the world. You are connected with them because you share the same goals based on tasks and milestones set by your organizations. What is challenging is that these teams have diverse management practices, leadership styles, communications traits and patterns, and decision-making bureaucracy. All these diverse team aspects can lead to numerous trust-oriented challenges, such as demotivation, conflict and crisis, frustrations, confusions and lack of commitment and participation. Apart from this, teams also face culturally rooted problems, which stem from either lack of relationship building or lack of task-oriented direction.

Other than that, you have no detailed information about the members you are working with. There are also some members who are not "pulling their weight." They do nothing, they say nothing! Yet letting go of a member may be difficult, especially when you are already reaching the last few stages of completing your tasks. However, retaining members who are not cooperative, committed or playing a role based on the goals set by the organizations can be as painful as letting them go. Decisions need to be made, and actions need to be taken. Whatever outcome you obtain will depend largely on the spirit of the members as a team.

Trusting others will also be based on the grounds of individual and cultural decision-making processes. In Asian cultures, people trust others when they have strong relationships with them, and thus the decision to work with another is based on affective dimensions such as feelings and relationships. During first encounters, people will take time to get to know each other. For example, in a team scenario, members will exchange personal information to allow others to know them.

Information such as their organizational backgrounds, past jobs and current status and roles, and family backgrounds are all counted as personal information exchanges during the "warm-up," or introductory, period. People determine a high need for relationship formation because, from their perspective, it will eventually lead to a trusting work environment, and, as a result, will induce a trustworthy colleague or team members. Therefore, the relationship orientation process needs to be nurtured and oftentimes given priority over task orientation. This condition is applicable in collectivist cultures, such as Asian cultures.

On the contrary, trust is observed differently in Western cultures. Decisions are made based on instrumental measures, such as if the other has demonstrated that he or she is competent in carrying out a task. Even if a relationship is built and a task cannot be delivered, one has no issue expressing dissatisfaction and is not fearful of harming the relationship. The reverse is true in Asian culture: People will make decisions to protect the relationship first, and then deal with the tasks.

Thus, managers need to understand which aspects are important in their own business cultures when making decisions, who is affected, why choices are preferred and selected, and how decisions are implemented. In essence, different people employ different rules for the choices they make based on different cultural measures and factors.

CASE BLOG 7.8

Faez: Indeed, you believe in me!

When Naomi, one of my global virtual team members, trusted me to submit the draft and final project, I doubted myself. Although she asked me to be a representative of my team, she is much older than me and I was sure that she would do better than me. I was afraid to make a mistake when I followed the steps to submit the draft and final project. Apart from that, I was so proud that Naomi thought that I was capable of doing it. So, when Naomi trusted me to do this, I tried to give my best without disappointing her. After the submission, I kept sending her emails to update her and she thanked me. I am so happy about this. At first, I had bad impression about Naomi. She was so critical, like most Americans, and she appeared to have no humorous side. At the same time, I understand that we need to be serious at particular times in order to perform our jobs effectively. By the end of the project, however, I liked the way she communicated with me. Even though she is 36 years old, she still asked my suggestion and involved me in the discussion. She believes in me. This is totally different from Asian culture, where we have to respect and ask suggestions from the older person first.

CASE BLOG 7.9

Choon Mooi: Trust is essential … and mutual

One of the team members said he was afraid he could not do well on one of the tasks. My response was that we all believed that he could give us an excellent outcome. In the end, he achieved success in the task. After this, the level of trust came to a high point among our team members. Let me relate my experience on trusting people in teamwork. I always finished my task earlier than the due date and shared it with the team before submission. I attempted to establish commitment by setting a specific time for discussion. However, one day the time was not suitable for me because of an emergency. I then proceeded to attend the discussion rather than deal with the emergency. I told my team members the truth about this, because I wanted them to know I am a person worth believing in. Communicating openly was an important part of building trust among the team members. In the beginning, we each discussed our strengths and weaknesses in regards to studying. For example, the American girl on our team said her mother language was English and therefore she could contribute by correcting our English errors. The Brazilian guy on our team said he was good at using technologies such as Google Docs and Dropbox, so we relied on him to solve our technological problems. Also, the girl who came from Croatia was good at collecting data, which was very helpful to us. Overall, with such openness, we put high trust in our team members to do things which were based on their specialties.

CASE BLOG 7.10

Nurul: The rollercoaster of trust

My level of trust in my members fluctuated over the 10 weeks of the project. There were team members I highly trusted at the beginning of the project because I perceived them to be trustworthy as Americans. This is because my knowledge of Americans was that they are normally high achievers. However, as time went by and we were working on the weekly tasks together, my level of trust in them decreased, as they were not at all like what I was expecting. They tended to procrastinate and to be less proactive than the other members coming from other countries. At first they showed interest to help, but then they did not try hard to cooperate with other team members. There was a time when we arranged a meeting that would be held according to their time zone and availability in the US and the rest of us had to stay up all night until morning; however, none of the Americans ended up showing up. This lack of cooperation was kind of frustrating and discouraged me from completing the task. After that, whenever we had a discussion, we just simply left them out and then just waited for their response when they came online. On the other hand, there was one of my group members whom I was unable to reach in the beginning, who explained that she had limited Internet use in her area. At first, I was worried that she was not being truthful. Yet she consistently tried to respond to us, although not frequently, and she managed to get all her tasks done on time. She showed her commitment by trying to get Wi-Fi anywhere she could. It seems that my perception of trustworthiness was different for each member at the end of the global virtual teams' project.

CASE BLOG 7.11

Rosmilawati: Be friendly

In order to gain the trust of others, I like to be friendly with them by not forcing them to do anything. I ask their ideas first, and then I make sure to be the first mover in the group and finish my part early. After that, others will follow what I have done and put their efforts in to add something that I missed to the report. For me, being a first mover and working hard to complete the report will show others how I take the project seriously and that I can be trusted. What can others do to gain my trust? The thing that works is for them to show me their efforts towards a task, even in doing only small little things. I also put my trust in them when they give me brilliant ideas and support my statements in the report. When I see this, I believe that they can do a great job.

CASE BLOG 7.12

Albert: Willingness is a virtue!

I have repeatedly demonstrated an ability to delay selfish gratification for small temptations. For example, I have worked through the odd hours (3 a.m. to 5 a.m.) or taken on onerous or tedious tasks that need to get done but no one else wants to do. As a team, all of us built strong bonds of trust by assisting each other even when we were busy with other tasks or assignments. I believe that teams build trust by engaging in off-site retreats that test their cooperative inclinations through participation in demanding tasks. As a suggestion, to regain others' trust, you have to be seen as willing to do what others might not in service of the company's larger goals, for example, putting off a planned vacation to meet a major need or goal of your boss. It is all about why and how much people are willing to take up the extra mile when others simply turn their backs on you for the extra burden!

BLOG VIGNETTE 7.6 Should I Tell the Truth, or Not?

Sharon was confronted with a difficult situation a few weeks back. The question was whether to tell her close colleague, Nelya, the truth – that she had made a decision not to follow through her recommendation, or to continue to tell her, "Okay, I will do it." To be precise, three weeks ago, Sharon had announced some good news (in her eyes) to Nelya, telling her that she would take up a new project and that the project was something she had wanted to work on for a long time. With a smile on her face, Nelya proposed that Sharon collaborate with Wahed from their university, who she said was an expert. After brief thought, Sharon agreed to her suggestion. Yet, a few days later, Sharon remembered an unpleasant incident she had had with Wahed in the past, which made her think he was not committed to research work. She then decided to forget about Nelya's suggestion.

Over the next few weeks, Nelya bombarded Sharon with endless questions about when she would take up her proposal, repeatedly asking, "When will you make that appointment to meet with Wahed?" At first, Sharon said she was busy; perhaps once the term was over she would set an appointment. She did not want to tell Nelya that she had decided not to work with him, out of fear she would pursue another line of questioning and ask, "Why not?" Nelya did not know of Sharon's negative experience with Wahed, nor did Sharon feel comfortable sharing this information with her. It is not Sharon's style to criticize or spread gossip about others. As the weeks passed, Nelya asked Sharon about Wahed again and again, finally looking at her busy whiteboard schedule, she said, "I noted your February and March deadlines – when will you make that appointment?" At that moment, Sharon became very irritated and annoyed. To her, her personal schedule and matters such as whom she will work with or not work with are very private.

The only reason she had shared her thoughts and intentions about this project with Nelya at all was simply to share good news, nothing more than that. She did not expect harassment or nagging over what she was supposed to do or not do. Sharon never thought her personal decisions would be an open discussion for others. Instead of telling Nelya she would not work with Wahed, however, Sharon finally said to her, "Okay, I will do it." Nelya asked when, and Sharon replied, "When I have the time." Nelya left the room. Sharon was relieved and thought that was the end of the discussion. Later, however, she had lunch with Nelya, who unexpectedly probed her further, "When will you meet Wahed?" Sharon was holding her breath and calming herself as the question raced through her mind whether to tell her the truth. Fortunately, she has become close to Nelya over the past few months, a factor that helped her make a quick decision of how to respond.

Finally, after three more nagging questions of "When will you do it?" Sharon told Nelya that she would only meet Wahed when and if she was free because she did not think it necessary to see him. She said she had only informed her of such decision to take up this research project in passing, and that she felt fully capable of completing it by herself because she had been doing this type of work for many years. Sharon emphasized that she was able to handle it without assistance, although Wahed was an expert. Nelya didn't buy the story. In the end, Sharon told her politely that she would not discuss the issue with her anymore.

So why is it that Sharon took so long to tell Nelya the truth? Nelya is a person who is dear to her now, and they have reached a level where their relationship has blossomed. Yet, from Sharon's perspective, Nelya forgets sometimes that there are certain boundaries one should not cross. Only months before, Sharon remembered a situation where she had behaved in an opposite way to Nelya and avoided crossing her boundary of privacy. Nelya had come to her office at the time with a worried face and asked whether she should collaborate with an American colleague. She was looking for advice and asked many questions:

You were educated there and you have worked with them, right?
What is your advice? How do I start communicating with this person?
Should I send her the email first or wait for her email? What do I write?
Do I ask her right away about the new project and the research grant available?
Or do I get to know her first? Hmmm, she is a stranger to me, you know!
How can I trust her?
This is difficult for me and I have never worked with anybody without meeting them first!

Sharon sat with her and tried to calm her down, knowing Nelya was excited over the idea and did not want to miss such a research opportunity. After giving her some tips, Sharon told her, "Go for it and stop worrying!" Nelya then walked out Sharon's office with a smile of relief and thanked her. Weeks passed by without Nelya mentioning to Sharon what had happened, nor did Sharon ask further about the subject. To Sharon, her principle was clear: if the matter did not arise or was not brought up again, then it was not her style to ask about it. To her, it is an *unstated rule* that matters should only be discussed when they need to be discussed. Otherwise, it is none of her business to ask about an issue, let alone to ask repeatedly. Nelya had come to her as a confidant, to seek her advice. Sharon therefore took her questions as personal matter, over which Nelya trusted her to pour out her anxieties; hence, she kept the subject personal and private. According to Sharon, this boundary should not be crossed, neither for her nor for Nelya.

CULTURAL LESSON 7.6: RESPECT ONE'S PRIVATE BOUNDARY

Let me begin this section with the predicament of a colleague that demonstrates the cross-cultural nuances of telling or not telling the truth. This situation allows me to use a cultural lens to provide an understanding of a dilemma which could easily arise in any workplace. What is interesting in this case is that according to Sharon, she has demonstrated a behaviour that appears to be a mix of Asian and Western culture. This is likely because, like me, according to Sharon, she spent a significant time working and studying in the United States. In Asian culture, confrontation is not favoured as an approach to dig out about someone's private matters. In the Asian culture, for example, if I were to come across people who behave as Nelya does, I would call them "nosy." It is also hard to say no to nosiness, and the more people probe, the more you feel pressured to cave in. At the same time, once a person becomes part of your in-group (i.e., the people with whom you have developed a relationship), they feel more comfortable expressing their thoughts, opinions and feelings. That is why your auntie, your uncle or your cousins can pop a sensitive question such as, "Why aren't you married yet?" or your favourite next-door neighbour can ask you, "What are you earning in Dubai?" When considering that Sharon sees Nelya as a close friend, it is then surprising that she did not confide the truth to her as part of her in-group. This may be because of her American experience of keeping a firm boundary between what is business and what is personal.

According to Trompenaars and Hampden-Turner (1997), the boundary of privacy can be further explained through a dimension called specific vs. diffuse. In a culture such as the American culture, people clearly set different boundaries between work and their personal lives. If you are at work, personal relationships are observed as mere extensions of your work, and these relationships are expected to carry no impacts on or consequences for the roles and tasks for which you are responsible. In other words, work is work, and friendship is friendship, and those two aspects are not intertwined in any way. The way workers look at things in this context is exemplified by the words, "I trust you to carry out the roles and tasks given, and personal matters should be set aside." People are therefore expected to be detached from one another and objective and rational in their decision-making and other matters at work. Another philosophy commonly observed among people in such a culture is, "When you are at work, you are my colleague or you are my boss; outside the office, you are my close friend."

In Asian cultures, the opposite is true. The boundary of privacy is intertwined and diffuse. Most of the time, the line between what is public and what is private is blurry, making it easy to cross this line and to allow work and personal agendas to have one goal. For example, a close friend could ask you to grant a favour in the workplace, such as overlooking a deadline she cannot meet, and you are obliged to be flexible to honour the friendship. To Sharon, this incident was not a question of being honest or secretive, it was about putting a clear line between her private and public space, despite the fact Nelya was her close friend. If you are in Sharon's shoe, I am curious to know what your decision would be. What strategy would you have chosen?

CASE BLOG 7.14

Kamilah: Use intermediaries such as email and SMS

Recently I have been through a similar experience, where my friend requested me to do something I was 100% sure I did not want to do. Yet I couldn't say "no" immediately to her request; I just didn't know how to say it. After that, she was calling me every day to remind me, and I got fed up with her calls so I started ignoring them. But then she began sending me SMSs day and night. After a few weeks, I really felt annoyed, as I continued to receive a number of missed calls from her. The reason I ignored her was to let her feel and understand that I was not willing to fulfil her request. Yet she never stopped calling me and rather kept pushing me to do what she said. I think in the third or fourth week, I decided to tell her that I was not willing to do what she requested; but I couldn't say it directly, so I sent her an SMS saying, "My friend you are not getting what I mean by ignoring your calls. I'm not willing to do what you requested." She replied and apologized, saying she was sorry and hadn't understood I was unwilling, and that she had just been trying to remind me. I felt a bit bad because I failed to say "no" from the beginning – this was an important lesson for me. Next time, I will try my best to directly say "no" in the beginning, because I don't want to experience the same consequences I went through in this situation. From this situation, I also found that we can use SMS, emails, and other intermediary forms of communication to say the truth we struggle to say directly from our mouths.

CASE BLOG 7.15

Noora: Just say it directly!

Although I come from a high-context environment and have experience in the low-context environment, my personality tends to favour the low-context style. I myself don't like the idea of a question after a question, that is, nagging. I don't know why; for some reason it irritates me. So for the situation illustrated above, my feedback would be to be direct, by simply saying from the beginning "It just wouldn't work out with Wahed" or "I decided to do it alone." See, if you want something to stop, it will never stop until you put a limit to it, so better to end that situation with a simple sentence or word such as "No!" At the same time, people won't know that you are trying to avoid a situation unless you explain to them your own personal behaviour by pointing out what you like and what you don't like, and what is acceptable and what is not. Otherwise, the discussion will be left open and close personal relationships will just lead to more open questions; so better to just point out the truth with good humour, because the facts have to be said. Just say the truth in an indirect and respectful way which results in your friend simply understanding with no further questions. Trust me, you will be haunted forever if you don't throw out a sentence with this effect. Don't take the 1-2-3 steps, just be direct and hit it on the spot; then you'll be free!

CASE BLOG 7.16

Junnah: Honesty is key

A similar experience happened to me with my dear friend asking invasive questions that left me with stress and an uncomfortable feeling. As a result, I approached the situation with honesty and being forthcoming, which eliminated a lot of stress and set certain boundaries with my friend so she would know she should not get involved in private matters. In addition, a friend should understand that there are certain personal matters and individual secrets that do not need to be shared or conveyed, even with those who are close to us.

CASE BLOG 7.17

Khaseefah: Establish boundaries

When I first moved in and met my neighbour, who is originally from a high-context culture, I was very excited, as she was from the same age group and I found her full of dynamism and many other qualities which were inspiring to me. Although I am from a low-context culture and not used to being surrounded by people who suddenly share their emotions or speak up their minds even if you haven't asked for them to share, my neighbour used to come very often to my house and share her problems. At first, I didn't mind, even though I usually avoid going to other people's houses unless I am formally invited. However, over time, I realized she had taken the freedom to take advantage of my silence and generosity by pestering me with inappropriate comments about my private life, ranging from my relationships, to items in my house, to my eating habits and many other things you would not want anyone else to be consciously aware of! The point is that I got very annoyed with this ungrateful person because she and her family (who also started welcoming themselves to my house and making themselves comfortable for hours without ever being invited) would intrude too much in my life, asking funny questions and being totally offensive!

CULTURAL REFLECTION 7.1: TORN BETWEEN BEING A BOSS AND FRIEND

Autonomy and authority lie strictly with the boss. One should obey the commands made, and one should listen to the boss. High power distance cultures are based on hierarchical, bureaucratic processes. Therefore, the separation between friendship and professionalism should be aligned correctly. I suppose the answer all depends on the cultural lens you use to analyse the situation.

- So, in that sense, was Anuksha right in having her secretary call Nina instead of herself?
- Perhaps Nina is the one who needed to adapt to her own work culture which embeds a hierarchical structure?

- Should Nina be disturbed by Anuksha's unwillingness to deal with her directly? If yes, why, and if no, explain the reasoning based on culture.
- What lens would you use? High power or low power distance? Is Nina's perception right here, or is Anuksha's way of dealing with the situation acceptable?

CULTURAL REFLECTION 7.2: CHOICES AND TIMING WHEN MAKING DECISIONS

When a person is facing a dilemma in a decision-making process, many questions arise. Reflect on this key situation when you are dealing with a client who comes from different culture from yours. You need to quickly close the deal, as the time frame to deliver the goods desired by the client needs a good amount of planning. But, the culture that you are dealing with observes time in a non-urgent manner. Time can be delayed. Deadlines can be postponed or people employ an attitude of procrastination. Thus, how do you respond to these questions?

- What would you do? What kinds of actions would you take to speed up the process?
- How hastily do you make decisions? And how calculative are you when doing so, i.e. making decisions?
- What rules do you rely on – the facts or the emotion you put into the situation?
- In what ways does the timing of making decision affect the outcomes of your performance?
- Can you persuade people to make decisions based on a relationship-oriented or task-oriented manner?

CULTURAL REFLECTION 7.3: TO TELL OR NOT TO TELL?

In the workplace, we will often be confronted with a situation that warrants us to make decisions and take actions. Sometimes we are faced with cultural dilemmas in which it is challenging to decide whether to tell or not to tell the truth.

- Why do people decide to be secretive?
- What are the cultural reasons underpinning "secrecy"? Provide several aspects of information boundaries and explain a situation that illustrates them.
- In what ways does culture influence or impact privacy or disclosure behaviours?
- How do you decide that "it is all right" for you to disclose information to others?
- How do you decide what kinds of information could be disclosed? For example, what about private vs. public information?
- To whom could you disclose private information compared to public information?
- How do you perceive risk when the information is "private" in nature or what you call a secret to be told?

CULTURAL REFLECTION 7.4: WHAT IS IT LIKE TO TRUST A STRANGER IN GLOBAL VIRTUAL TEAMS?

In contemporary organisations, people are assigned to a team in a novel structure called "global virtual teams" (GVTs). However, the specific challenges of working in a GVT could include:

- Waiting up during the late or wee hours of the night to have a Skype meeting with your colleagues in another continent when you've already devoted a good 9 to 10 hours at the office that day.
- Working with people who regularly miss deadlines because they perceive timelines as flexible and adjustable according to their schedules.
- Working with people who keep their silence when things go wrong, because they feel they should try to solve a problem until it can no longer be fixed.

The strange thing is that, even after you have worked with your team for more than a few weeks, you feel like you only got acquainted last week because trust was not established. The big and underlying questions here are:

- How do you quickly develop trust among the team members during the inception stage?

- Do you think trust is crucial at the early stage of teamwork? If yes, why and how does trust influence your performance? If not, why?
- Does trust matter to you in teamwork based on relationship or task orientation? Can you explain and provide examples?
- You realise that, even after weeks 3–4 of working together, you still know nothing about a team member, other than the tasks they are assigned to. What will you do to enhance the relationship? What will you do to earn trust from your team members?
- Is there a boundary between work and friendship when you collaborate with others on a team?
- How do you perceive the relationship between trust and privacy?
- In what context is it important to respect privacy, and under what circumstances can privacy be breached? Can you explain, based on your culture?

7.1 @CULTURAL PONDERS

My Pledge: Once I Say Yes, I Will Deliver!

Timothy Sean
Autumn 2010

Ever since I read Abdullah's blog, it made me think. It is mind-boggling to me ... why and how people could say something, then decide differently, and consequently act differently? For instance, you said, "I promise" to a friend who has asked you for something, even though you can't do it – but in order to not make him feel bad, you will nod and say, "Yes." This is so very different to my culture. I don't believe it is better or worse, just different. In my culture, if you say, "I promise," and do not deliver – you have lied. You have said you will do something and not done it. This causes people to lose their credibility and their reputation is tarnished. People do still promise things they cannot deliver – but the word will spread very quickly that this person cannot be trusted. If I was in your shoes and a friend asked me to promise something and I knew that I could not do it – the friend would expect me to say no. To say, sorry – I can't do that. Yes, it will make him feel bad – but he will appreciate the honesty and openness. I suppose it must come back to my culture being very direct and very blunt. If I can't do something, I will say so – openly and directly. I would think the person I am speaking to will appreciate my honesty, rather than just saying something to make them feel good. Whereas in your culture, Mohammad, the person would appreciate the gesture and take it that you care enough to try your best. Very different – and clearly problems will occur. If you promised something to me, Mohammad, when you could not do it, I would feel as though you have let me down. On the other hand, if you asked me for a favour and I said, I'm sorry, I would like to but I cannot – you would probably take offence to it and think I don't care. Very different but very interesting. Culture does influence the way we communicate our intention and our actions which lead to effective decision-making.

8

Culturally Attuned Global Leaders

Leaders become great, not because of their power, but because of their ability to empower others.

John C. Maxwell

BLOG VIGNETTE 8.1　What's It Like to Be a Global Leader in Dubai?

Imagine this scenario: an expatriate employee working with an expatriate leader. How's that? On one hand, it does feel like a rollercoaster with many variations of approaches, styles and values, which is perplexing and disconcerting. On the other hand, in a positive light, in Dubai I am living in a truly cultural *salad bowl* as I experience different flavours of leadership which has enhanced my cultural intelligence. But how can you make sense of the leader whose culture is totally different from your own as they craft a different path? And who says leading and leadership are easy?

The continuous and debatable question is: Should leaders be moulded into a culture via training (nurtured), or should leaders be accepted with their naturally born traits (innate)? Thus, the characteristics and values that come as a package should be appreciated as they are. That is the real challenge of working in a multicultural hub like Dubai. You make your choice, and you stick to it, even though you might be leading workers from a different culture!

I live in a country which has the reputation as "Truly Asia" that is commonly filled with Malays, Indians and Chinese. For decades, we have embraced diversity and multiculturalism, both at work and socially. I have had the opportunity to work with leaders from three different races without reservation because, after all, we are Malaysians. We are tightly bonded by similar cultural values, but there are disparities based on our races and religion.

When I arrived in Dubai, it seemed the workplace scenario was utterly different. Everywhere you walked and everything you saw revealed immense cultural diversity. Why? Dubai is home to more than 200 nationalities. Having lived in Dubai for quite some time, it makes me think: if Dubai's workforce is fuelled by expatriates, this means you have a high chance of being led by an expatriate from another culture. Even so, the chances that you will lead people from more than three nationalities in one department are highly conceivable.

CULTURAL LESSON 8.1: MOULDING A CULTURALLY ATTUNED LEADER

Once you're in Dubai, you'll realise you're *waking up* to a city bursting with expatriates. You'll also become conscious that expatriates proliferate exponentially as the year passes. One might ask: Why are there so many expats in Dubai? The reason was reported in the local newspaper, *Gulf News* (March, 2018), by Mercer's 20th Quality Living Survey: Dubai is ranked the best city to live in in the Middle East and Africa and 74th globally in overall quality of living. Dubai is known for its modern and digitally equipped infrastructure, safety, security and health facilities. By 2030, it is expected that Dubai will have an astounding number of expatriates living and working in all sectors. What does this imply for you as part of the global workforce in terms of leadership? A key question that arises is: What is the possibility of being led by an expatriate and working on a team of expatriates? The answer is that almost 80%–90% of the global workforce in Dubai will experience such a work scenario of working side by side, hand in hand, with expatriates of more than 200 nationalities.

No surprises. No exceptions.

Thus, should the expat leader be moulded into a culture relevant to the people he or she will lead? Or should the people who will be led become the ones that should be culturally adaptive? Indeed, should the leader become invulnerable to culture, because everyone and anyone is culturally different to the extent that culture doesn't matter? What matters most is to work well with heterogeneous teams, albeit a monoculture. I've worked with many bosses who are culturally different from me in my years of working in Dubai. Cultural values do make a mark on how the leader sets the tone for the organisational culture and shapes the values, attitudes and norms in the office. Why they say what they want, how they send messages and the platforms they choose have a huge impact on one's leadership style.

Communication and other management practices also matter, for example, the way a boss negotiates a task within a team. What approaches do you employ that will get your team to agree to commit to and engage with your message? Confrontational vs. avoidance? How about decision-making: Do you empower your team to think outside the box for them to decide what the best solution is and act upon it?

Or do team members simply share information and deliberate with others, yet the final say, the final decision, needs to be routed to the boss because of a hierarchical culture? What about the urgency of time: How do you perceive time? Will the leader set the tone for meetings with the principle of "Time is money!" and must deadlines be stringently adhered to? Or does the leader convey that time can wait and thus people can multitask, procrastinate and/or delay the timeline given? These complexities and cultural paradoxes influence how leadership style is developed and how training facilitates expatriates to become culturally intelligent leaders.

CASE BLOG 8.1

Mohammed: A good leader needs to be a role model

In order to develop this image of "leaders are not born but created," I think any leader throughout the globe willing to succeed in his role needs to practice first the approach of taking the lead without dominating. In this regard, he should be very receptive to whom he leads in his organization. Listening to them and appreciating their suggestions and opinions can show how he encourages his team to contribute for the sake of developing the organization. Going further, he shouldn't imagine himself being without mistakes, as no one is perfect... even in Dubai! For sure mistakes are just part of polishing the path to successful leadership. I remember a couple of months ago when I complained to one CFO in a major financing company about a certain policy he had approved. He astonished me when he replied, "We shall review this policy." After a couple of days, I was informed about amendments concerning that policy. He took initiative for the sake of everybody in the organization, which I appreciated. Above all, a good leader needs to be a good model. This can be seen in his commitments and beliefs, his practices and approaches. Frankly saying, Sheikh Mohamed of Dubai holds the above qualities, and many more. He is a leader with vision that brought Dubai to accomplish huge achievements, without sacrificing a lot, through understanding what people from other cultures appreciate. Accordingly, he made miracles that others are still trying to replicate, but have not.

CASE BLOG 8.2

Maleena: A global leader

At some stage, a few years ago, there was this crazy hype going around the UAE about leadership and how to be a good leader, and so on. The statement "How to be a good leader" hit the UAE in a way that seemed there was nothing more important to focus on. I suppose the reason for this is the new rise of an open-minded and exposed generation. In our world today, the phrase "I don't know" does not justify your lack of knowledge, as everything is now open to us and can be easily accessed by us. A leader isn't someone who can just guide you and motivate you and push you to achieve certain goals. A leader today is someone who has the courage and the patience to go down to your level in order to make you understand and motivate you and make you achieve the best outcome you possibly can.

Nonetheless, a successful leader today *has* to be a global leader, not just a leader. This means someone who is open to and is literate about other cultures and nationalities, that is, someone who is cultured. A person can be a great leader among his circle of friends, but when you put him in a multicultural organization, his leadership skills become a mess because the people he is leading are new to him and, on top of that, they come from different backgrounds. When placed in a situation where you could lead a group of people from different cultures, one needs to educate oneself about two very crucial things: how to be accepting and how to be patient. I do believe that each one of us has at least one leadership skill, but it is up to us to develop ourselves and become better leaders, not just to others but to ourselves as well. But what leaves me puzzled when it comes to this whole leadership talk is one thing: Why do we strive so hard to become leaders who are culturally attuned? I mean, why is it a good thing to become a leader?

CASE BLOG 8.3

Michael: Charismatic leadership

The interesting thing is that leadership can take so many different forms. Some lead by example, some lead using power – the different techniques are vast. When a situation requires charismatic leadership, it is very difficult to teach someone how to be charismatic. I think people are either charismatic or they are not. You cannot put a person who is not charismatic in a situation that requires charismatic leadership and expect him/her to succeed. Take Barack Obama, for example, or probably any U.S. president for that matter. The U.S. president has to be charismatic to be successful. He has to be able to motivate people through his speeches and actions; his ability to "rev" people up is crucial to his success. President Obama, in my opinion, is very charismatic. Putting a person who isn't charismatic in his shoes is unlikely to be successful. Now this doesn't mean that this person cannot be a good leader – not at all – it just means that he doesn't have the leadership traits to do this particular job. He may thrive in a different leadership positions – perhaps one that requires "leadership by example," or a position where his/her skills and knowledge effectively lead the people around him/her. In summary, I believe that leaders can absolutely be made, but not in all circumstances, and leaders who are born leaders will thrive in circumstances where others simply cannot, not matter how much they try.

BLOG VIGNETTE 8.2   Do Leaders Need Talent or Experience?

The phrase "Leaders are born, not made" is frequently heard in the workplace. Yet many contemporary corporations believe that leaders can be trained and developed over time through many effective leadership training programs. Some people think that the characteristics and charisma of a leader can be identified in children as young as seven years old. I remember from my primary school days a boy named Ahmad Nubly. Whenever he said something in class, other kids listened and did what he said, willingly, and without force. He was always in the limelight among his classmates and became an influential figure at a very young age. He often attracted a crowd of girls and boys, and had many admirers because people found him very funny, credible and warm-hearted.

On a different note, the student who was our class monitor, Moses Tan, had a serious look, yet was polite and kind, and whenever he gave instructions in our teacher's absence, all of us obeyed. We were terrified of his tone and acknowledged his superiority and authority. It is amazing to reflect on this memory of more than 40 years ago and how it shows that different styles of leadership can be equally effective – even if they instil entirely different emotions in followers. It also makes me realize how some people are born to be leaders, as both Ahmad and Moses were. Others, of course, nurture and develop the characteristics of a leader over time, after years of observation and experiences. Still others fail to become leaders even when placed into such a role at work.

And so, my question is: Can leaders be nurtured to have similar qualities as those who are *born leaders*? Could we replicate and mimic the exact charisma, traits and personality inherent in a born leader? How about the cultural make-up of the leader that we are mimicking; for example, can a leader from Canada be moulded and trained into a Chinese leadership style and vice versa? Intriguing phenomenon, but it is a real challenge to envision the shaping of a culturally attuned global leaders.

CULTURAL LESSON 8.2: LEADERS ARE NOT BORN, BUT MADE?

The illustration of my childhood memory of Nubly vs. Moses also shows that different styles of leadership can be equally effective. In Asian countries, society accepts the inequality of power distribution. The boss is the one who directs and instructs others. In this kind of environment, known as a high power distance culture, power and authority are clearly displayed and openly applied to others. When a boss reprimands, he is sending the message "I'm the boss, I'm in control here." This is a custom and practice that everyone follows and agrees with. In the United States, on the other hand, which is a low power distance culture, a subordinate feels free to disagree with the boss's decisions, and the boss usually doesn't have a problem with that as long as it is done professionally and courteously. From a young age, American kids are taught to say what they think, to be truthful and honest, and clearly express their opinions and feelings. Asian kids, on the other hand, are raised to obey and respect their elders, meaning keep quiet and listen. Being polite and humble are core cultural values. So, what does it take to become a leader today, especially in a virtual environment?

From another spectrum of global leadership, I would like to pose two key questions:

- What kind of global talent with the right leadership skills should human resource managers seek?
- What kind of cross-cultural training is right for you as a global leader managing multicultural teams?

A colleague of mine works at DU, the biggest and most prestigious telecommunications firm in Dubai, composed of 30 nationalities of employees. Another colleague of mine working at Hewlett Packard, Dubai, mentioned he has at least five different nationalities of colleagues in his department. Each person brings myriad forms of cultural values which are paradoxical. Indeed, cultural values present challenges to manage and coordinate. It seems to me you should have skills that allow you to rotate with 360 degrees of cultural knowledge! Besides, imagine the kinds of diverse training that you need to develop as effectively and efficiently as possible to fit with your global talents – comprising multitudes of cultural backgrounds.

CASE BLOG 8.4

Jaber: Focus on human relations

Whether the leaders are born or created, they should be able to adapt to a people-oriented leadership style in order to successfully confront the challenges of being managers in a multicultural workplace. Besides the importance of being culturally competent and having a high level of cultural intelligence, leaders should be focused on human relations with their employees. Being people oriented, leaders should strengthen their relations with employees to the extent that they (the leaders) will be able to eliminate any misunderstandings created due to cultural differences, ensuring seamless communication. The stronger the personal relations among the employees and their leaders are, the smaller the cross-cultural barriers will be.

CASE BLOG 8.5

Zahirah: It's the team that leads, not the individual

I do agree that leaders are made and not born. This is why to study successful leaders, you need to take into consideration the big picture. In most countries around the world, a successful president or prime minister appoints his/her own team and people that he/she has been working with. I think no one can argue that a large part of President Obama's success was due to his campaign team. The point is that a successful leader *must* have an expert team supporting him. In other words, it is the team that leads, although it has a front man/woman who is responsible for the overall result. Having said that, *it is a team that leads, not an individual.* Although the vision and route map are usually created by the leader and he is considered "the brain" of the operation, I believe to be able to be generate the best results, any leader must bring with him his own team and people that he/she has confidence in.

CASE BLOG 8.6

Jovish: Big personality

I think that a leader should be aware and have a wide vision of the environment around him so he can mould himself according to that environment in a way to use the right channels to interact with subordinates from different cultures. So, I think that leaders are created and not born, as they will be created according to the medium that shapes them. Moreover, the strengths and weaknesses of a leader's personality will have a big effect on his subordinates, and vice versa. I think that the personality plays a big role in creating leaders and their traits.

BLOG VIGNETTE 8.3 "I Order You to…" or " I Ask You to…"

One of my favourite movies is *Bicentennial Man*, with the title character played by the late Robin Williams. The movie tells the story of a sentimental robot who eventually becomes part of a family, full of love, compassion and affection. The robot wants so badly to be human and one day, after years of serving, the robot seeks approval from his master to be free. His master says, "So you want to leave us?" And the robot says, "No, I just no longer want to be ordered around." With a shocked look, the master explains that there is a difference between "ordering" and "requesting," and says that his is the latter. Ironically, the robot says, "I want to be free but I am always here to be of service." The thing that always strikes me about the movie is the concept of command/order vs. request/plea. It helps me to reflect on the issue of this week, which is leadership or management style. In the early days of management (the 1960s and 1970s), the organizational form was based on a tall and hierarchical structure. People were ruled by higher orders of management – instructions were top down. Then, in the 1980s, the organizational form began to change to a flatter structure, and we saw the birth of the concept of "empowerment" in which direct instructions (orders) are less frequent. Instead, people are freer to do their jobs and are held accountable for their own decisions.

CULTURAL LESSON 8.3: MOULDING A LEADER FOR A CULTURALLY ORIENTED ENVIRONMENT

In management books on effective leadership, authors often suggest that a manager who can motivate is a person who can inspire people to do their job based on willingness and understanding. As illustrated in the above movie, the master said "you have the right to make decisions. I am not ordering you but I am requesting. You can say no." In contrast, in an Asian culture, this condition may not prevail because the decision of whether to follow instructions all depends on the leader's asserted power and authority, to the extent an employee or subordinate will readily admit that "I follow orders without discussion, even if and when I don't agree, because you are the boss!"

I often wonder what constitutes a good leader in Dubai. Maybe I should rephrase the question as, "What constitutes a good leader anywhere?" More specifically, what makes a good leader in today's borderless world, where there are multicultural employees to be led? We have reached the seventh week of class, and every week when we discuss our topic, I ponder this issue afresh. How do we behave as leaders now, in this global world? And how might we lead and manage employees in Dubai? Consider the following scenario: An American CEO is sent to a subsidiary plant in Thailand, where he must lead hundreds of employees. Serious cultural barriers exist between the American boss and the Thai workers. To ensure success, the American boss's organization should provide training on how to deal with and appropriately manage Thai people.

CASE BLOG 8.7

Mashael: Everyone deserves respect!

Leading your employees with an "I order you" approach is not right, or at least, I think it is not right. As a leader, your leadership should be respected and accepted ... we are all human beings and should be treated with respect. When you order a person to do something, you are not giving him room for an opinion. When you request, however, he can still say "no" and there will be a place for an opinion and argument. For example, in a financial investment company, when it comes to a very basic or practical task, an order is a better choice. When the task is something negotiable, then a request is a better option so there will be room to negotiate and share feedback on a complex issue. However, there will be exceptions, depending on the organization we are dealing with. The case of a financial firm may be very different from a construction or garbage disposal company. As well, your approach may also have to depend on the mentality of the person you are dealing with.

CASE BLOG 8.8

Lateefa: Family-oriented

In my opinion, leaders are born and then they can be shaped to become even better leaders, because they already have the right traits. Such leaders have the power of personality and the knowledge and skills that allow them to affect and influence others. Their influence persists forever, even after they leave their position. And these leaders are few in number because today companies are trying to create leaders and, to my knowledge from my workplace, these created leaders last for few years and then when they leave, no one mentions them anymore, because their achievements were not impressive and they have not left an effect on the employees or the community. To me, a leader should create the feeling of family within a team, even though the members are from different societies. His/her vision should be one for all, which means all members of the society or the organization feel they belong and are involved in reaching this vision. His/her power is to encourage and not threaten others. A leader should thus not hold high power distance, so that he/she reaches all members of the family, in order to understand and communicate with them.

CASE BLOG 8.9

Nasser: Effective teamwork

Leadership is a pathway, and a natural position more than an administrative one. Leaders are not born to be effective leaders, but they are created and developed through years of experience and training. Leaders need to have open and attractive communication skills, which make them "influence" others, and are more a part of their personality. When the leader can influence others and always be in touch with them, up to date, he will unite everyone, who will welcome his advice, opinions, ideas and so on.

In all workplaces, not only in Dubai but also in the whole world, companies are looking to build effective teamwork and comfortable working environments to satisfy their inside customers (employees), leading them to satisfy outside customers (consumers). Leaders should be committed to the vision of the organization and know how to use and deliver the information when needed. In Dubai, it does not matter from which country the leader is coming, but rather the way he deals with and treats other workers, the way he convinces people at higher managerial levels, and the way he influences his team members.

BLOG VIGNETTE 8.4   Yes, I Listen Since You Are the Boss!

Today, in Dubai, the work scenario is even more complex. A multinational organization might send an expatriate manager to Dubai, where he or she must lead and manage not only natives of Dubai but also people of many nationalities; the employees are multicultural, not monocultural. The challenges are therefore multiplied in terms of cultural confrontations and dynamics between leader and employees. We are no longer talking about a leader whose staff is only locals, known as "Emiratis," in Dubai. Instead, we are talking about a foreign manager leading many nationalities under one roof, under one organizational umbrella. Or we could also consider an Emirati leader supervising workers from many nationalities. How do we train and develop a global leader capable of effectively confronting such challenges? What are the traits and behaviours necessary in a global leader who must adapt his management style to accommodate the different work cultures of people from all walks of life, each with their own cultural values and their own personality?

CULTURAL LESSON 8.4: CERTAINLY, CULTURAL INTELLIGENCE IS NOT AN EXCEPTION!

From an organizational point of view, what are the challenges in creating these new global leaders? As I have said in the early illustration in this chapter, leaders are not born but made. So, what is the new mould for leaders who must manage and lead people in Dubai? What framework and what models are inherent in this new and interesting workplace? I'd like you to share with me your thoughts, experiences and aspirations about working in

Dubai, the challenges of meeting people from 160 nationalities, or if you are working in any multicultural workplace, anywhere in the world.

For myself, I was constantly exploring and seeking new answers when I first came here. It was a new environment for me because I was no longer educating students of one culture but rather students of many varied cultural backgrounds. I thought my flexibility and knowledge of diverse cultures was sufficient, but they were not at all. People have their own perceptions which shape their mental models. It is difficult to fully interpret and predict behaviours because different perceptual schemas lead to different emotions and behaviours. Cultural intelligence is needed to allow a person to make sense of cultural situations and experiences. Cultural complexities and paradoxes cannot be well managed without knowing and understanding the assumptions of a specific culture. Moreover, lack of cultural experience will result in misinterpretations and miscommunication. Hence, I am still learning.

CASE BLOG 8.10

Valery: What is the effect of personality on leadership?

In my opinion, leaders are born leaders. I was recently reading about the Big Five Personality Model and I was thinking about myself. Definitely a good leader should possess many qualities mentioned in this model, but those are personality traits that are inherited at conception. A successful person should be an extrovert personality, that is, very sociable, pleasant and easy going. But what if you are at the other end? If you are an introvert, or not agreeable, or if you sustain stress poorly, or are not flexible, then what? Can you still be trained to become a great leader? The answer is yes and no. If we look at Barack Obama, he didn't emerge from nowhere. As a black man, he struggled to reach where he is today. His biography is very interesting and tells a lot of his extraordinary personality and great achievements. I think it is easier to spot individuals with leadership traits and then, with good training and experience, to enhance their performance, followed by investing time and recourse to train employees who don't have the potential to become leaders.

CASE BLOG 8.11

Saad: Leaders need to be moulded!

Recently, I attended a presentation on leadership, which I really loved, and would like to share it with you all. The presenter mentioned three categories of people (related to leadership) and they are as following:

1. Two percent of people are born as leaders and you can notice this from their childhood, and thus the speaker recommended to take care of them as talented individuals;
2. Ninety-six percent of people are born as normal people and they can gain and improve their leadership skills from experience and training to develop culturally intelligent leaders;
3. Two percent of people cannot be leaders no matter what they do, even with training and experience.

So, I agree with the statement that leaders are mostly trained and moulded, but a small percentage of them are born leaders.

CASE BLOG 8.12

Haitham: Good leaders are made, not born

If you have the desire and willpower, you can become an effective leader. Good leaders develop through a never-ending process of self-study, education, training and experience. There is a difference in ways leaders approach their employees. Positive leaders use rewards, such as education, independence, etc. to motivate employees, while negative employers emphasize penalties. While the negative approach has a place in a leader's repertoire of tools, it must be used carefully due to its high cost on the human spirit. Negative leaders act domineering and superior with people. They believe the only way to get things done is through penalties, such as loss of job, days off without pay or reprimanding employees in front of others. They believe their authority is increased by frightening everyone into higher levels of productivity. Yet, what always happens when this approach is used wrongly is that morale falls, which of course leads to lower productivity. Most leaders do not strictly use one or the other style, but are somewhere on a continuum ranging from extremely positive to extremely negative. People who continuously work on the negative side are bosses, while those who primarily work on the positive side are considered real leaders.

BLOG VIGNETTE 8.5   Can You Really Nurture a Culturally Attuned Leader?

A key question about contemporary leadership is: Can leaders be culturally nurtured, or must leaders be born into their own natural habitat, that is, where their leadership can emerge naturally from their own environment (culture) at a young age? Is leadership a talent that arises from modelling what they see in people around them? Can an American successfully lead a Japanese team or a German or a Thai team?

Many of my students in Dubai have commented leaders should be moulded to fit different cultural needs, depending on whom they are leading. Someone once said, "It is difficult for people to change when they reach their mid to late 20s." Yet, at that age, most people are just beginning to climb the corporate ladder; they're getting their first management experiences and building themselves up for higher-level leadership roles. How is that possible if they can no longer change? How can they be trained to become a leader?

This irony requires further exploration of the concept of interculturally competent leadership. A *request* is a form of asking, and one has a choice whether to do it. But an *order* is different: it's a command or instruction. No choice, no negotiation.

It's true that, at some point in our work life, we'll feel like a robot, particularly when we're obliged to follow instructions, even unwillingly. So, what about your boss? What's his or her style of leadership? Orders or requests? What's your leadership style?

Remember, we aren't judging whether the style is a good one. The most important thing is to understand the culture in which the management or leadership style is rooted.

CULTURAL LESSON 8.5: ARE WE CULTURALLY COMPETENT?

So, if we were to use a culturally theoretical lens, we could understand how power distance plays out in different cultures. In the last few years, I read an interesting column in *Friday* magazine (published by *Gulf News*) entitled "Natural Born Leader." The article highlights a well-known behavioural psychologist named Adrian Furnham who discussed the "natural-born leader" as opposed to the "nurtured leader."

Dr. Furnham provided an interesting perspective on the ways leaders can be shaped and the ways they are naturally talented. He mentioned that leaders are not only concerned about themselves, but rather, they want to motivate and inspire their staff at work. And that is a major task.

In my opinion, the ability to inspire and motivate people sets apart the leader from the mere manager. A manager needs to function at the operational level, while a leader needs to function at the strategic level. Dr. Furnham continued to say that, as a leader, you should "start by understanding yourself and what you need to work on and why." He also said culture influences leadership systematically. Conversely, he observed that people hold similar values and beliefs about what constitutes a good leader, despite their varying cultural backgrounds.

This statement got me thinking: If cultural differences don't really shape a leader, since all leaders have the same aspirations (i.e., to motivate employees to fulfil their mission), can culture still affect leadership style?

Maybe I should pose the question another way: How are we supposed to nurture and develop interculturally competent leaders capable of confronting and dealing with a multicultural workforce? There are seven areas that we need to focus on if we wish to create interculturally competent leaders:

In Table 8.1, there are seven leadership dimensions that we need to focus on if we wish to create interculturally competent leaders and ways to fit in based on the relevant cultural context, as suggested by Zakaria (2017). These seven dimensions provide key guidelines for strong and powerful ways to mould global leaders to lead multicultural teams in multinational organizations.

TABLE 8.1

Seven Global Leadership Dimensions for Culturally Competent Leaders

Leadership Dimensions	Cultural Context
1. Cultural Immersion	• Ability to acculturate to a new environment • Ability to appreciate the strange things around the new work setting • Ability to engage with people in order to develop new friendships
2. Capability	• Possession of the necessary leadership skills, both in qualifications and experience • Preparing three kinds of competencies to acculturate effectively: cognitive, affective and behaviours • Emulating the right behaviour as leaders when managing multicultural teams
3. Care	• Ability to be compassionate, to express empathy for and care about the well-being of those whom they lead • Ability to acknowledge emotions both at the level of self-awareness and others
4. Connection	• Ability to interact effectively with a variety of people, develop relationships and make connections easily • Ability to sustain the relationships with good ethical values as well as relational intelligence
5. Consciousness	• Awareness of one's surroundings and of the changes in one's environment, particularly when dealing with cultural diversity • Awareness of how culture influence behaviours – both for self and others.
6. Context	• Possession of a well-defined perspective for developing measures and strategies to cope with a GVT's cultural dynamics
7. Contrasts	• Ability to compare cultural factors based on different countries and in different organizations • Ability to compare cultural dynamics in teamwork • Ability to predict cultural influence on behaviours at individual level

Source: Zakaria, N. 2017. *Culture Matters? Decision Making in Global Virtual Teams: Managing the Challenges and Synergies during Globally Distributed Collaboration.* CRC Press, Taylor & Francis Group.

CASE BLOG 8.13

Khassefah: No perfect fit for a leader

A leader should remain the most charismatic figure of an organization; however, leadership styles vary from one culture to another and, further, defining leadership style remains very challenging, as the definitions vary from one context and situation to the other. Currently, I have so far been very fortunate to work in a flat organizational structure, where my directors, from the United States, have been tremendously friendly, open and kind with me. Indeed, given the current challenges in the market, my directors have definitely demonstrated all the abilities of great leaders which have helped us to expand the business throughout the country. In fact, as a trainee, I have been able to learn a lot from them because of their excellent communication skills. Because they are straightforward – to the point and gentle in formulating their requirements, even when giving urgent orders – I have always managed to receive them very well and hence meet their expectations. For this reason, so far everything has been running smoothly throughout the company, with no one complaining about our bosses, particularly because all of our ideas are either welcomed or discussed if not everyone agrees. Hence, the leaders in my company have definitely been leading through requests rather than orders.

CASE BLOG 8.14

Suraya: Ordering in a decent way

I truly believe that a good leader is created and not born to be one. A person could have leadership qualities, but these qualities will dissolve away if not strengthened by proper training, experience, dealing with difficult situations and, most importantly, the inner willingness to improve and change for the better. I personally come from a high-context culture with high power distance, and this culture is dominant and obvious where I work. Whether he orders us or requests us to perform tasks, our manager usually says "Could you please do this...," so he is basically ordering us, but at the same time in a decent way. He somehow is able to create a sense of urgency (which is required in finance) and even when he is not around, things are always completed in a timely manner. The qualities that make a leader stand out from others are being able to make employees understand the importance of the well-being of the organization and simultaneously be the thinking mind of the organization.

CASE BLOG 8.15

Akarsh: Learn, adapt and keep growing

Taking into account that I came from India to study in Dubai, subsequently succeeded in getting a job here, it's an interesting environment to work with varied cultural styles. In the process of completing my postgraduate study, I have met good 'buddies' in college and tried to gain first-hand knowledge on their culture. When I stepped into a company in Dubai, meeting colleagues from different regions and countries, again I have learned multicultural styles of work. Now, this experience has shaped how I would like be a leader: to know what my work and goals are, then learn to offer my network of friends and colleagues a level of comfort (i.e. by learning their approaches to life/career), then move along with them on the same wavelength and prosper in whatever I do. If we look at how my cultural background is going to contribute to my leadership style, I would say both my cultural and leadership styles would be to: learn, adapt and grow.

BLOG VIGNETTE 8.6 Who Is in Power?
Hierarchy and Leadership

In Asian countries, society accepts inequality of power distribution. The boss is the one who directs and instructs others. In this kind of environment, known as a high power distance culture, power and authority are clearly displayed and openly applied to others. When a boss reprimands subordinates, he is sending the message "I am the boss, I am in control here." This is a custom and practice that everyone follows and agrees with. In the United States, however, which has a low power distance culture, a subordinate feels free to disagree with the boss's decisions, and the boss usually doesn't have a problem with that as long as it is done professionally and courteously. From a young age, American kids are taught to say what they think, to be truthful and honest, and clearly express their opinions and feelings. Asian kids, on the other hand, are raised to obey and respect their elders, meaning to keep quiet and listen. Being polite and humble are core cultural values. So, what does it take to become a leader today, especially in a multicultural and global virtual team environment? If we were to analyze orders and requests using a cultural theoretical lens, we could understand how power distance plays out differently in different cultures. Let me reinforce the idea that a *request* is a form of asking where one has a choice whether to do it or not. But an *order* is different – it is a command or instruction, with no choice and no negotiation.

CULTURAL LESSON 8.6: WHICH ONE IS AMENABLE? HIERARCHICAL VS. FLAT STRUCTURE

While a flat organizational structure is prevalent in Western culture, contradictorily, in Eastern cultures, the hierarchical form is still very much in existence, though we were discussing the emergence of the flatter structure here in Dubai (from this week's presentation, e.g., DU, Emirate Airlines, etc.). So, what is the leadership style? Is it autocratic, participative or consultative? We saw that in Dubai, many organizations use the consultative leadership approach, where inputs from subordinates are taken into consideration before making decisions. However, though input and deliberation takes place at every level of the organization, at the end of the day, the final decision still comes from the boss. In the autocratic style, on the other hand, instructions come straight from the highest levels of hierarchy. Please note that the phrase "I order..." has a different ring in different cultures.

In Asian cultures, for example, when a boss asks you to do something, most of the time it is in reality an order. Why do I say that? Because in a subtle way, the boss's words are as good as an order (unstated rule), an instruction or a command. *What the boss says goes (so to speak).* I often heard my colleagues and heads of departments in my previous organization sigh, "We've just got to do it," or, "It comes from the top management, hence it's not open for a discussion." We were often frustrated, but we just followed instructions as employees.

For instance, I once asked my Asian-culture Dean, "Do we have to follow what was instructed without any questions?" With a brief answer and half-jokingly, he replied, "Oh Yes, I am the dean!" We also read from many books on effective leadership which suggest that a manager who can motivate is a person who can inspire people to do their jobs based on willingness and understanding. There is no such thing as, "I follow orders without discussion, even if and when I don't agree." How far is such phrase applicable in the context of your workplace and in the cultural context that it is embedded in? It is a mystifying endeavour when you are dealing with cultural nuances that could potentially affect one's leadership style. It is the push and pull factor between organizational culture vs. national culture. It is only you and your team who can make that choice in terms of how you want to shape the organizational culture through the roots of your own cultural values.

CASE BLOG 8.16

Eiliyah: Learn to be a leader who is culturally sensitive!

In my opinion, some leaders are born leaders naturally, some leaders are nurtured culturally and some are learning how they can be leaders. In our modern world, globalization is an important issue, and its consequences are inevitable. One of these consequences is the challenge of managing multicultural organizations. To be a successful leader, if we are not born naturally to be a leader, or we are not nurtured, we should try to *learn* to be leader. According to

Prof. Adrian, "it is difficult for people to change when they reach their mid to late 20s," but he didn't mention it is impossible. It absolutely takes time to learn to become a leader; it is a long process, but it is possible. In Change Management, I learned that, according to Alvin Toffler, "the illiterate of the twenty-first century will not be those who cannot read or cannot write, but those who cannot learn, unlearn, and relearn." Also, there are some models and theories about personal change which can help us to become better leaders. In Dubai, because of its multicultural environment, first leaders should be aware of different cultures within their organization. Then, they should learn about becoming a global leader who is more flexible, tolerant, patient and adaptable. In short, "continuous learning" is a very important and a vital issue on an individual and organizational level in the twenty-first century.

CASE BLOG 8.17

Jamila: Environment shapes a person, as much as culture

In my opinion, the context in which a person is raised and educated has a big influence on polishing his or her character. Culturally, a person can be influenced by the environment he was raised in, especially when it is an environment that allows individuals to express opinions and lead others to accomplish certain tasks. Different cultural exposures, grouped with care for others and conscious motivation of others to grow, complete the essence of becoming a leader. Also, resolving conflicts between individuals in the same working environment allows leaders to take advantage of cultural contrasts and build bridges that promote coherence and connectivity within teams. A leader is a social worker, a cheerleader, manager, and globally oriented individual, with a vision and strategic goals to be achieved.

CASE BLOG 8.18

Saaedah: Change is inevitable to realize your dream!

I believe that when someone wants something, they should do whatever they can to get it, so change is in the hands of each individual person. Mainly, it is not about changing, but rather learning to adapt to a particular environment. We have all reached a point where were believed "no, we can't," but the truth was "yes, we can." It is all in our hands if we are optimistic enough and willing to do so.

In the end, you are still you and there is no change in that. That's why, in such decision-making, we, as women, need to be masculine, and it is important to understand that our role at work is different than our role at home. This phrase fits into both articles: the one featuring Dr. Furnham, and the one that mentioned "a leader should be a piece of clay that could be made into any shape to fit anywhere." Developing such flexibility requires many years of experience – not so long, but long enough to learn the risk of every corner and to gain a vision of the world as a whole in terms of its culture, people, organization, professions, levels, jobs, tasks, advantages and disadvantages, technology and more.

Since I was young, I have dreamt of becoming a successful businesswoman. This is my long-term goal and vision for the future. I believe that one day I will be able to, in sha Allah, reach that point, as it suits my characteristics of being a good debater and problem solver, as well as a person whom my friends can open up to, trust and somehow rely on, and a person who can cheer up and fight. Being only 23 years old, I still have a long way ahead of me to gain knowledge and experience, and I cherish every moment of learning something new!

CULTURAL REFLECTIONS 8.1: HOW DO YOU LEAD MULTICULTURAL TEAMS?

Imagine one day you are assigned to lead a large project which you are expected to complete in only three months. Imagine that your team is multicultural, with members from all over the world. Imagine that their working styles and the ways they communicate are very different from one another and from your own. Finally, imagine that the team can only collaborate in a virtual workspace – that is, through Skype, Facebook, Whatsapp and other web-based tools.

- Where do you begin?
- What do you say?
- How do you instruct, monitor and lead such a team?

CULTURAL REFLECTIONS 8.2: WHAT'S YOUR LEADERSHIP STYLE?

So, what about your boss? What is his or her style of leadership? Does he/she lead through orders or requests? Remember, the purpose of this discussion is to identify the *style* of a manager. We aren't judging whether the style is a good one. The most important thing is to understand the culture in which the management/leadership style is rooted. When you manage your team at work, based on this phrase "The boss is still a boss," what are your thoughts given the few key questions below?

- How does culture influence leadership style?
- How can you be an effective leader?
- Do you mould yourself to suit the objective or goal or to suit the conditions or context in which you are working?
- Are good leaders born or made?
- Can we mould ourselves into effective leaders by reflecting our own unique cultural makeup, or is it independent of our cultural roots?

CULTURAL REFLECTIONS 8.3: WHAT DOES ALL-ROUNDED LEADERSHIP LOOK ALIKE?

The challenge today in Dubai or any multicultural society is that leaders need to be as wide open as possible in heart and mind to be able to accept all the possibilities of cultural complexity. *Reflect on this situation.* You have just been appointed to head a group of multicultural expatriates in your conglomerate company. You have an MBA that focused on global leadership, and now is the time to apply such skills. Over the next month or so, a new project worth millions will be handed to you with this team. Several questions begin to arise:

- What is your own self-evaluation of your leadership traits?
- Are you ready to lead – to motivate and influence people from a variety of cultures and walks of life, from all corners of the world?
- Are you ready to be open to the many idiosyncrasies of behaviour, the turmoil of emotions, the unpredictable patterns of thought and mind shifts in a multicultural environment?

At the same time, there is another set of key questions:

- Can leaders be culturally nurtured, or must leaders be born into their own natural habitat, that is, where their leadership can emerge naturally from their own environment (culture) at a young age?
- Is leadership a talent that arises from modelling what they see in the people around them?
- Can an American successfully lead a Japanese team, or a German or Thai team?

8.1 @CULTURAL PONDERS

Leaders, Be Authentic in Your Actions and Approaches!

Najwa Mahmood

Autumn 2010

I always believe that "a confident man walks like a king." You don't have to be rude to be a good manager because Hitler died and his dictatorial age finished a long time back. In today's companies, the usual structure is the hierarchy one, where the most powerful position in the company is at the top of the pyramid. If the manager is smart enough, he will use his position in a way that benefits everyone in the company. He will talk, share and advise all staff. He will listen to new ideas and thoughts and never underestimate anyone in his organization. He should inspire the employees to give their best in what they are doing. In contrast, there are some kinds of managers who prefer giving orders and never listen to the employees. They believe that they are the smartest and nobody should prove them wrong even if they are! I will tell you a story that happened to me and was the main reason for my leaving my previous company. Our CEO was very tough; he only gave orders, and sometimes I felt that I was in the military and not in a government-civil organization. Everybody used to be scared of him and never argued or negotiated with him except me! I was the black sheep; I always negotiated with him and explained to him and even proved him wrong if he really was. I feel that is the normal relationship between the manager and his staff. I have a bold personality; I didn't care if he was the most powerful person in the organization or not. What mattered to me was that the work was conducted smoothly and without sensitivity or problems. He should have known that we were working with him, not for him! I was patient until I felt that he would never change and my organization was going nowhere with a CEO like that. I couldn't live in Hitler's age and pretend that I was in 2010. Therefore, I preferred to move to another organization. In the interview with the new CEO, instead of him interviewing me for the job, I was the one who was interviewing him. I wanted to make sure that he was a healthy man. The atmosphere in my current organization is very healthy and normal, as the CEO is a great leader. The bottom line is that the old-fashioned way of managing people in organizations is absolutely wrong and has proved to be a big failure for any manager who is trying to make everyone believe that he is the one! People now are smart and can differentiate between the smart leader and the stupid leader who is trying to hide behind a dictatorial style to hide his weaknesses. Notably, Dubai is filled with expatriates more than locals and hosts a residence of more than 200 nationalities. With such a phenomenon, a leader needs to be global in his style, approaches and strategies to win the talent's hearts – an organization's main asset.

Section III

In Search of Global Talents with Cultural Intelligence

9

Building a Culturally Fit Expatriate

Learning to recognise and interpret cultural behaviour is a vital step forward for expats anywhere, but it doesn't mean that you grow to appreciate all the difference.

Sarah Turnbull

BLOG VIGNETTE 9.1   Laila, You Are One
Intelligent, Culturally Curious Kiddo!

As usual, when my husband and I take a lift to our apartment, meeting new people is a mixed experience. For the past two years, we often have bumped into countless expatriates. We're not prepared to know the best way to greet people, nor do we know how we'll be greeted. Whilst some smile pleasantly, some look away. Others have a blank expression. But this morning, the lift opened before us with cheerful smiles from an Arab family of five: a parent with three beautiful kids and a nanny. We reciprocated such joviality with pleasant faces and warm smiles.

As I was grinning at the three-year-old girl, I asked the mother whether she was going to the beach on a beautiful Saturday morning. She said no; instead, they were going to the clinic. Not wanting to be nosy, I left the statement at just that.

As the lift opened to our floor, the eldest daughter asked a question with glowing eyes. "Where are you from"?

"Guess where I'm from," I teased.
"Indonesia," she replied.
I responded, "That is my neighbouring country."
The father nodded and immediately said, "Malaysia."
Laila didn't hear our brief exchanges, and as the lift's doors were
    about to close, she shouted, "So, where are you from?"
"Malaysia!" I repeated.

Afterward, my husband's immediate reaction was, "She is so good in her geography, yeah!" How could she not be? She had correctly guessed which continent we hailed from. She keenly observed us to make sense of our culture, she seemed to appreciate and value differences, and she reacted very quickly in search of truth. In my view, she is certainly curious about culture, and she is harnessing her culturally intelligent capabilities at a very young age. If she is so agile culturally, why can't we adults be equivalently agile and attentive?

CULTURAL LESSON 9.1: WHAT DOES IT TAKE TO BE CULTURALLY INTELLIGENT?

Earley et al. (2006) defined cultural intelligence as "a person's capability for successful adaptation to new cultural settings, that is, for unfamiliar settings attributable to cultural context" (p. 5). In short, a culturally intelligent person can deal with cultural nuances. An expatriate who wants to be competent in their job while they are abroad needs to develop this cultural intelligence; if they go into a situation without any prior knowledge or experience of the culture, they are likely to be blind to the myriad cultural attitudes and characteristics that shape the behaviours of others, and cultural blunders are likely to ensue, including miscommunication and misinterpretation. Simply put, an expatriate possessed of cultural intelligence is more likely to be equipped to adapt to and work in a multicultural environment. Also known as cultural quotient (CQ), cultural intelligence comprises four main elements (see Table 9.1).

For multinational corporations, these four elements are the crucial skill sets and cultural competencies they need to be aware of when recruiting and training global talent. Earley et al. (2006) saw them as prerequisites for global managers, who need to recognize the various factors that impact expatriates' initial cross-cultural adjustment. Expatriates experiencing prolonged or severe culture shock may struggle to recognize the positive aspects of their host culture when they first arrive. The role of the global manager is to minimise this culture shock so that expatriates can move swiftly on to the adjustment and mastery stage.

In the initial stage of adjustment, expatriates will begin by exploring observable behaviours, as expressed through artefacts and symbols. My fashion dilemma as an expatriate in Saudi Arabia is a simple example. As a newly arrived SIE at the Riyadh Airport, I had many unresolved questions: Why were all the local women wearing long black dresses and headscarves and the men all wearing long white traditional dresses? Why did the *abaya* only come in black and white and not in other colours? My initial feeling of strangeness was compounded by the realization that I was out of step with everyone else, and the fear that I would not be accepted if I didn't conform to the dress code. Coming from Dubai, where women wear *abaya* in a range of (subtle) colours, I had to learn about Saudi expectations regarding women's fashion, and this gave me a deeper understanding of clothing as an artefact. Equipped with this knowledge, I had to make the strategic decision whether to dress in the same way so that I would be more readily accepted in the

TABLE 9.1

Key Elements of Cultural Intelligence

Cultural Elements	Key Questions	Short Quotes from Respondents
1. *Cultural knowledge*: Capture the facts of the culture, what we should know about the culture, and how things operate, from what we observe.	What do I know about this? • Values • Systems • Leadership	• I was expected to make decisions instantly, but I was not empowered to do so! • I was informed that relationship orientation breeds more trust than task orientation.
2. *Cultural thinking and learning*: Metacognition, or how we think about culture ("thinking about thinking"), and how we understand what we learn.	What do I think and how do I solve problems? • Planning • Awareness • Checking	• I am pleased that people are expected to demonstrate what they can do (performance) rather than who they know (connections/network). • I am keen to get involved and participate in the decision-making process, and not wait to be instructed.
3. *Cultural drive/motivation*: The ability to be connected to the culture, learn and be confident and appreciate the culture.	Am I energized? Am I motivated to do something here? Am I persistent in my actions? • Extrinsic motivation • Intrinsic motivation • Self-efficacy	• I am motivated to work towards collective goals. • I want to take risks and meet the challenges posed in the workplace. • I favour working with people from different cultural backgrounds. • I am confident I have the skills and knowledge to socialize and team up with multicultural workers.
4. *Cultural actions*: The ability to respond relevantly and appropriately to the situation encountered.	Can I do the right thing? Can I take certain actions? • Verbal • Nonverbal • Speech-acts	• I have observed that people communicate in a direct manner when they describe a task. • I have learned that timely decision-making is important, not delaying it. • I see people tend to say "Yes," but they don't keep their word.

Source: Earley, P. C. et al. 2006. *CQ: Developing Cultural Intelligence at Work*. Palo Alto, CA: Stanford University Press.

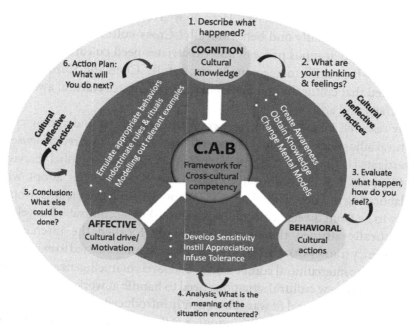

FIGURE 9.1
The CAB cross-cultural fit model for building SIEs cultural competency.

country. This strategic thinking led me to take the culturally appropriate action of mimicking the host country's dress code. The four elements of cultural intelligence thus interact to create a process that is cyclical and dynamic in nature (see Figure 9.1).

CULTURAL LESSON 9.2: THE COGNITIVE, AFFECTIVE AND BEHAVIOURAL (CAB) INTERCULTURAL COMPETENCY MODEL

A culturally intelligent expatriate needs to ponder on several questions such as: Am I able to manage encounters that are culturally challenging? Do I often make cultural blunders because I don't understand the situation? Am I able to readily diagnose a situation and accurately read my own and others' emotions? If people answer these questions half-heartedly, they are experiencing a cultural dilemma. Essentially, the key question people should ask is: Am I culturally fit? Organizations which are keen to recruit

SIEs should also ask themselves: How do we recruit global talent that is fit mentally, emotionally and behaviourally? Cross-cultural adjustment is a long-term and arduous process, and expatriates need cultural intelligence and know-how skills to negotiate it successfully. Chen and Starosta (1996) suggested that culturally competent managers requires cultural awareness, sensitivity and adroitness.

My research focuses on the impact of culture on SIEs undergoing cross-cultural adjustment. Drawing on several cross-cultural theoretical lenses to investigate (1) the cross-cultural competencies needed for global managers as SIEs, (2) the intercultural communication styles SIEs adopt when collaborating in a new workplace, and (3) how SIEs and their teams (who are likely to be from diverse cultural backgrounds) co-acculturate, I developed a culturally attuned theoretical framework I called the intercultural competency framework (Zakaria, 2008). The framework aimed to explain and describe the intercultural competencies and levels of intelligence that people experiencing new cultural situations need to handle at work and in general. The concept of cultural fit was subsequently introduced into the framework, which was renamed the CAB (Cognitive, Affective and Behavioural) cross-cultural fit model (Zakaria, 2017). The framework proposes that there are three dimensions of cultural competency: cultural awareness (C), cultural affective competency (A) and cultural behavioural competency (B). These dimensions are interdependent and complementary. SIEs are also required to have cognitive ability, emotional responsiveness, strategic thinking and appropriate action orientation (knowing how to behave).

In essence, SIEs need to have the complete CAB skill set to adjust effectively. A culturally intelligent SIE is cognizant of their own and others' culture, sensitive to and tolerant of diverse cultural values, and able to learn to behave in ways that are compatible with the host culture. SIEs who are able to achieve a high level of cultural awareness appreciate and are sensitive to cultural nuances, and consequently emulate the right behaviours. Most expatriates realize that the journey of expatriation involves encountering multidimensional challenges that require different types of competency. Learning how other people think, feel and behave needs cultural competencies, skill sets and intelligence (Figure 9.1).

Without exception, expatriates are expected to demonstrate cultural competency, but developing this competency is not easy; it requires SIEs to know themselves as well as others. SIEs also need to understand that for certain competencies, some facets are more important than others. Likewise, in certain facets of adjustments, all three competencies are needed. Some people might have contradicting values which influence how SIEs undergo cultural expeditions, that is, the timeframe taken and the strategies to be employed.

COGNITIVE COMPETENCY: KNOWLEDGE AND AWARENESS

Understanding cultural differences usually begins at the cognitive level. At this initial stage, knowledge about the new culture needs to be fully assimilated and understood so that the prospective expatriate is aware of the basic differences in terms of food, climate, language, geography, time and so on. This cognitive process also includes establishing self-awareness and cultural awareness – learning about oneself and others. When the expatriate first enters the host country, they only perceive culture at a surface level. Since their perceptions and thoughts are guided by their background knowledge of the newly met culture, these will depend on how much they have learned and where they obtained their information. The more things they don't know, the more they become unaware of the cultural effects, that is, things they do not see or anticipate in terms of the consequences.

To understand the culture, they must be alert to their surroundings and ask: "What is happening, and why is it happening the way it is?" For example, an American expatriate working in the Middle East or Asia for the first time may find it irritating when they observe that meetings with locals seem to habitually begin late, especially when these are official functions. At the cognitive level, they will develop a mental model, a perception that local people are laid back in their attitude toward punctuality. Such a perception activates the cognitive component of their competency. They need to be educated with the relevant general and culture-specific knowledge that becomes the basis for guiding their thoughts and perceptions. SIEs will make sense based on their perceptions and thinking.

It is important to provide information and support so that SIEs do not engage in sophisticated stereotyping; as Osland and Bird (2000) pointed out, human beings are complex and cannot be pigeon-holed on the basis of their observable or unobservable behaviours. Only through knowledge and raised awareness can stereotyping be avoided and SIEs engaged to understand and appreciate cultural diversity. However, this cross-cultural training is rarely available to SIEs. It is up to the firms recruiting SIEs to provide relevant and comprehensive cross-cultural training not just at the initial entry point but also throughout the adjustment process. This training must avoid creating stereotyping-oriented perceptions among multicultural teams. It is up to SIEs to develop their own cultural sensemaking so that they avoid making generic assumptions. A culture may represent a shared set of values, but this is not the same as saying "one size fits all." Culture is complex and people from different cultures most of the time have unexplainable behaviours with unpredictable emotional states which need to be discovered and uncovered. Culture needs to be explored more deeply through the different layers, as illustrated by the onion model and analogy (see Chapter 2). SIEs need to seek a deeper layer of explanations by developing a different competency such as cultural sensitivity.

AFFECTIVE COMPETENCY: FEELINGS AND SENSITIVITY

With cultural knowledge and inherent understanding, expatriates become more self- and culturally aware. With self-awareness, they can learn to better appreciate others' differences and predict the effects of their behaviour on others. Cultural sensitivity means being aware of specific cultural differences and similarities and how they affect values, learning and behaviour. It involves having the affective or emotional skills to look beyond the cognitive or logical level; for example, being able to infer meaning and interpret nonverbal communication cues such as facial expressions, body movements and gestures. As SIEs go through the different phases of adjustment, they will deepen their understanding of the symbolized behaviours and artefacts that express the host country's cultural values. Through their interactions with colleagues and/or society, they will become more knowledgeable about the culture and learn to understand culturally oriented behaviours and situations. As they become more knowledgeable, they should become more culturally sensitive, as long as they have some level of emotional intelligence (EQ).

Goleman (1996) identified four dimensions of EQ, two of which deal with the consciousness of self, and two of which are concerned with knowing others. Self-awareness is the first dimension of EQ; for example, expatriates must acknowledge what they feel when they commit a cultural blunder. The first step is to recognize:

- What types of blunders have you made?
- When did the blunder take place?
- Why did the blunder take place?
- How was the blunder rectified? Did you think about the mistakes made?

The next dimension is self-management, which is divided into emotional self-control, adaptability, achievement orientation and positive outlook. These aspects allow expatriates to make sense of themselves. In the CQ model, the metacognition level is described as "thinking about thinking." Expatriates need to reach more deeply into how they feel in order to better manage the emotions produced by culture shock.

The third dimension addresses social awareness, or how aware expatriates are of the society or people around them. Expatriates must recognize and empathize with the emotions of others, though asking someone how they feel, especially when one is in a new environment and they are strangers, is not easy. Recognizing someone else's emotions can also be made difficult because different cultures have different ways of communicating their emotions. Trompenaars and Hampden-Turner (1997) suggested that people face dilemmas in formulating cultural thinking strategies. Western cultures might adopt an affective communication style, openly expressing their feelings about an event or situation, while Asian cultures are more likely to keep their feelings to themselves in order to avoid confrontation. Knowing this cultural fact will help an expatriate understand how best to approach their colleagues from an emotional point of view. The last dimension is relationship management. Many criteria count, such as influence, coach and mentor, team and inspirational leadership. In essence, SIEs need to develop EQ if they are to relate to others in a meaningful manner and be able to put themselves in someone else's shoes.

BEHAVIOURAL COMPETENCY: ACTIONS, BEHAVIOURS AND SOLUTIONS

If they are to present culturally congruent behaviours, SIEs must have both general and specific knowledge about the host culture. As they acquire cultural knowledge, people learn to be tolerant, appreciative, responsive and open to the differences that are evident in individuals' behaviours. It is only when a person is equipped with adequate knowledge and sensitivity that he or she is able to demonstrate effective cultural behaviours. The fact that dichotomous cultural frameworks do not take into account context, personal beliefs and norms limits their usefulness when it comes to explaining the cultural paradoxes that are manifested in individuals' behaviours (Osland and Bird, 2003) (e.g., how an Indian may subscribe to collective values while simultaneously holding religious beliefs that ensure that he or she is individually accountable for his or her own actions). Accordingly, by gathering rich, descriptive evidence of SIEs' cultural behaviours, I have sought to understand how people's behaviors are impacted by culture.

Osland and Bird (2003) assert cultural behaviours are too complex to be described or explained using generic dimensions, such as those offered by cross-cultural theorists, including Hall (1976), Hofstede (1984) and Trompenaars and Hampden-Turner (1997). By reiterating what Osland and Bird suggested about the cultural intricacy and complexity manifested in people's behaviour, it becomes crucial to understand the role and impact of culture in light of diverse cultural experiences. Culture offers paradoxical elements that humans need to continuously make sense of in the situations they encounter. A lack of knowledge and sensitivity may leave an expatriate uncertain of what to say, what to feel and how to react in a given situation. If expatriates can avoid stereotyping, they will have open hearts and be able to tolerate and even appreciate certain behaviours and blunders when they experience them. Their adaptable perceptions and mental models regarding a given situation will prepare them to accept the complexity of culture. At this stage, SIEs need to be equipped with different skill sets and competencies that enable them to become more attuned to and appreciative of myriad culturally paradoxical behaviours. Ultimately, SIEs need to appraise behaviours based on whether certain practices are congruent with cultural norms. By examining situations from the perspective of cultural values, SIEs will be willing to model appropriate behaviours, and this compliance will lead to knowledge of others who observe such attitudes, characteristics and values.

CULTURAL LESSON 9.3: THE RULE OF THUMB FOR BUILDING CULTURALLY FIT SELF-INITIATED EXPATRIATES

Some people have reservations regarding the extent to which cultural competencies can overcome workplace dilemmas, particularly given that these competencies take time to develop. However, not developing them can ultimately be more expensive – for example, if the expatriate is so frustrated by continuing difficulties that they decide to leave. SIEs need to develop cultural competencies with care, patience, and diligence. Only with the right skill sets and cultural competencies, expats could undergo cross-cultural expeditions with positive attitudes, and strong faith and beliefs. The following guidelines allow SIEs to reflect on their own competencies, as defined in the CAB model (see Figure 9.1) and as outlined in the cross-cultural training modules to develop intercultural competency skills (see Table 9.2).

TABLE 9.2

Cross-Cultural Training for SIEs: Using the CAB Intercultural Competency Model

Cognitive Aspect: Know Your Culture, Don't Make Presumptions
- Create a positive mental model and mindset based on high cultural awareness.
- Be clear in terms of how you perceive situations from the initial observation; don't jump to conclusions or make any presumptions that are incorrect.
- Do not look at a situation from a single angle; look at it from multiple angles.
- Do not be judgmental or resort to stereotypes.
- Start searching for culturally attuned knowledge and information for guidance.
- Learn about others' values, attitudes and perceptions by observing what you see around you.

Affective Aspect: Feel for Culture, Learn to Appreciate Cultural Diversity
- Develop an enthusiasm for cultural diversity.
- Learn to tolerate different cultural practices, norms, routines and habits.
- Be sure to acknowledge and listen to your own and others' feelings without judgment.
- Appreciate differences through different ways of communication – verbal and nonverbal.
- Be sensitive to different values and acknowledge the uniqueness of others' attitudes and perceptions.
- Show warmth and understanding.
- Show compassion in challenging situations or when faced with cultural blunders.

Behavioural Aspect: Observe Culture, Emulate and Act Accordingly
- Observe the surroundings with a flexible mindset to recognize your own and others' cultural roots.
- Imitate what you have observed and be consistent in practicing it.
- Develop rituals and customary practices based on what you have learned from predeparture training and ongoing training, or based on information from colleagues, friends and family.
- Consider getting a mentor or coach who could guide you to inculcate behaviours which are culturally attuned.
- Involve yourself in cultural training to understand appropriate behaviours which are aligned with your thoughts and emotions.

CULTURAL LESSON 9.4: GLOBAL MIND, OPEN HEART AND CULTURALLY SAVVY BEHAVIOURS

Expatriates need to be prepared for a potentially bumpy ride. At first, they will inevitably experience confused thoughts, turbulent emotions and perplexing and unprecedented behaviours which may leave them feeling pessimistic about the whole enterprise, particularly in the culture shock stage. However, at the other end of the cross-cultural adjustment journey, they should emerge with a global mindset, an open heart and culturally savvy behaviours, all aligned to become culturally intelligent. The adjustment process is different for every expatriate, but it always involves them developing a more realistic understanding of the new culture and learning to recognize the similarities and differences between it and their home culture.

All SIEs need to develop cross-cultural competencies to be effective and efficient in their new workplace. Only if they are well aware of their "self and others" will expatriates be able to make sense of the cultural nuances and accept cultural differences with an open heart and mind. If they have a flexible mindset, they can learn how to replicate and mould their behaviours to suit the host culture, but if they fail even to recognize the importance of being educated about culture, they will find their cross-cultural expedition much more of a challenge. In today's multicultural work landscape, SIEs need to accept that cultural competency is no longer optional. A solid repertoire of cultural skills is essential not just to combat the cultural shock waves, negotiate change with confidence and master cultural upheavals, but fully to embrace the exhilaration and opportunities offered by the cross-cultural experience.

CULTURAL REFLECTION 9.1: MAKING SENSE OF CULTURAL BEHAVIORS

It is common for people to observe a situation and then try to make sense of its patterns of behaviours. What people do and why they do it may be explained to some extent by rituals and norms. The role played by values may be more challenging to discover, as these tend to be deeply rooted and entrenched. The assumptions underlying manifested behaviours may be uncovered with key questions such as:

- How do cultural values impact behaviours? Why do cultural values matter? How are they revealed to expats when they first enter a new work environment?
- How do expats take account of cultural values when they first enter?
- What kinds of practices need to be followed? What happens when these practices are not complied with?
- Can rules be changed in the cultural context? Should rules be aligned with the different cultural values, attitudes and beliefs?
- Do the cultural rules need to be followed at all times, or does it depend on the context?
- Do people learn about culture or culture-based rules over time and over generations? In other words, is culture inherited?

CULTURAL REFLECTION 9.2: CONFLICT OF CULTURAL VALUES

Let's reflect on a hypothetical work scenario which might lead to a conflict of cultural values. Many organizations have a dress code which governs what employees should wear. But what if this dress code is incongruent with one's cultural values? For example, Muslim women are required to dress modestly and cover their hair, but some airlines require female flight attendants to wear skirts that don't fully cover the whole leg.

- As a manager, what would you do? How would you advise a new recruit who wears a head scarf because this is in line with her Islamic values? Yet incongruent with the dress code outlined in the airlines?
- Would you take a stand to protect your employee and her cultural values, or would you ask her to follow the organization's or airline's rules on dress code?
- As an expatriate, how would you respond to this cultural dilemma?
  - How do you feel? What is your reaction?
  - Would you reflect on your cultural beliefs and values when making decisions?
  - What actions would you take to ensure that it is congruent with your values?

9.1 @CULTURAL PONDERS

Perplexed and Mystified? Observe, Tolerate and Act!

Maya Galiyeva
Autumn 2018

During their usual get-away time at the *Arabica* cafe, Maya Galiyeva proudly announced to her friend,

> "I need to be culturally vigilant!
> I need to be attentive,
> I need to be alert, and I need to be sensitive.
> In short, I need to be culturally intelligent!"

Culture is complex, culture is so unknown. I can't be blinded by things I don't understand. Diana Ibramagivo quickly responded,

> "Hmmm, what do you mean *cultural intelligence*?
> I have never heard of that word.
> Can you explain? I am fascinated!"

Maya began to tell her a story. "I accepted the challenge of becoming an expatriate in melting pot city like Dubai because I want the challenge of meeting diverse customers. Unfortunately, I was upset the other day when I tried to close a deal with one of my customers at the store. As a marketing manager at Louis Vuitton in the Dubai Mall, I manage hundreds of customers every day. I meet many interesting people, with widely differing tastes. Over five years, I have learned to accommodate their needs and understand what they want, and I am good at it. But, but, today, with this one incident, I was bewildered.

You see, Mr. Jerry Wong walked into the store and started to browse our latest collection.

As usual, I approached him with a bubbly tone:

> 'Welcome! How can I assist you today?'

He faintly smiled and continued to look through the collection without a word. After standing close to him for almost five minutes, I tried to engage with him again:

'What kind of bag are you looking for?
For whom are you buying the bag?
Do you have any preferences in color or material?'

With that question, he began to look irritated. He looked away and within seconds, swiftly left the store. I was puzzled at his demeanour because he was not as responsive as I thought he would be, and he didn't want to ask any questions. A few minutes before, I had been entertaining a European customer. Within seconds, he was bombarding me with questions regarding our Autumn collection. It took him almost an hour before he decided to purchase the latest design, but I was happy despite the long negotiation process. It was worth the time as I had managed to convince him to purchase our most costly Louis Vuitton. But with this Chinese gentleman, I was clueless. I didn't understand his way of communication or his body language." Frustrated, Maya quickly sipped her coffee before saying,

"Diana, I was blind and I was culturally ignorant!
I need to be culturally fit if I am to win the hearts of all my walk-in customers. *You see, I need to be culturally intelligent as I mentioned to you just now!*"

10

What's Next for Self-Initiated Expatriates?

As the world becomes flat, cultural convergence is the reality, wherein culture is lifeblood to an expatriate! Conceivably, we will continue to breath in a world full of flavors depicted by cultural uniqueness!

Norhayati Zakaria

BLOG VIGNETTE 10.1 Is it Really Culture, or Personality, or Human Nature?

I remember one postgraduate student Mikyle Duposu argued vehemently during a class discussion, "I still don't see how culture is an influential factor – I still think it is personality!" He said this on the day I asked the class to complete a questionnaire on decision-making styles. To him, decision-making had to do with personality. I said to the class that evening, "Let's look at our decision-making styles based on our cultural perspectives. Let's not narrow our minds to the individual and personal level; instead, let's open up our minds and explore other possibilities, look for other explanations, expand our awareness and understanding of what culture is all about and how cultural values can influence people's minds, emotions and actions." In this particular case, it was a challenge for me to convince Mikyle that *"Culture does count!"* Cultural roots penetrate so deeply, and often we don't even recognize its growth within ourselves. We often take it for granted, for instance:

- Why do you comply with an instruction given by your boss without question?
- Why do you keep silent when you disagree with a colleague, or with your boss?
- Why don't you speak up when you know you can't deliver a job on time?
- Why do deadlines matter more to some people than others?

Complexities arise not only from cultural values, but also from one's personality. But isn't personality built on culture, too? Talk about humans – aren't humans complex? Don't their desires, preferences and attitudes affect how they behave in the workplace? In a nutshell, we are all humans who are characterized by distinctive personalities and enriched by unique cultural values.

CULTURAL LESSON 10.1: CROSSING THE BORDERLESS WORLD WITH CULTURAL KNOWLEDGE

In Chapter Two, "Defining Culture," I conceptualize culture based on a pyramid structure and explain its meaning through three layers – personality, culture and human nature. My years of research have led me to see culture as sandwiched between our understanding of personality and human nature. An individual's personality is exemplified through one unique person's behaviour, while human nature is manifested in universal behaviours as observed from all people as humans. Then, what is culture representative of? Culture is the behaviours and values that are shared by a group or category of people, and it differs from one group to another. It is an innate process through which people learn how to think, feel and react. My question is this: "What are we without heritage and traditions, and who are we without values?" If culture is part of our history, and if history continues to shape our values and personalities, then personality too has its roots in our culture, and consequently cultural values shape personality.

In his prominent book *The Borderless World*, Kenichi Ohmae (1990) prepared multinational corporations (MNCs) to accept the global village as the reality of their workplace. He envisaged the world as becoming flat, and argued that cultures will converge as people are brought together by the similarities in their values, attitudes, and behaviors. Where there are differences, these will be accepted as the features that make them unique. Happy to live within a cultural melting pot, people will accept cultural diversity as a commonplace. SIEs have capitalized on the opportunities afforded by global mobility, moving from one country to another in pursuit of both tangible and intangible rewards. In the past, self-initiated relocation was not a common strategy for global talents due to a lack of cross-cultural training. Without sufficient training, cultural shock takes longer to overcome. As such, talented and potential global managers are reluctant to experience failures and take the risk of going abroad to work in a foreign workplace!

Unegbu and Onuoha (2013) argue that, with the effects of globalization and the Internet, many traditional workplaces are being supplanted by more advanced work structures as aptly mentioned by Kenichi Ohmae's second book (2005) entitled *The Next Global Stage: Challenges and Opportunities in Our Borderless World*. More opportunities are opening up as increased job mobility brings excitement, growth, achievement and challenge within the reach of global managers willing to try something new. The coming decade will continue to witness a rise in new forms of workplace and structure as these global managers move from one country to another and workforces become increasingly diverse in terms of cultural background, age, generation, educational background and profession. Transferring to a foreign country may be more lucrative than staying put in one's own home country, and relocation will be a popular choice for expatriates dreaming of a challenging career. However, the move to a new country requires knowledge, competency and intelligence.

BLOG VIGNETTE 10.2   Yes, Undeniably, It Is the Cultural Force!

With the dawn of globalization and borderless world, Kenichi Ohmae (1990) have long argued that culture is converging. Hence, people will share similar values, beliefs, attitudes, and act alike. However, as an SIE, how could I deny the cultural forces as evidently manifested at my workplace while living in Dubai? I am certain that many SIEs out there would not disagree with the notion of cultural power. Now that I get the opportunity to make sense of the cultural nuances, I am indebted to my students who work in various multinational and local firms in the United Arab Emirates. As promising SIEs, they offer their insights into cultural complexity and its impact in the workplace. At the end of 10 weeks of co-learning and co-sharing about cultural forces at work, all of them agreed that culture has an inexplicable but tangible power. Culture equally introduce incongruities as observed through people's multifaceted behaviors. In essence, culture slips into our daily lives in an observable manner, but most of the time, cultural behaviours are implicit and elusive, touching one's feelings, thoughts and reactions in a way we may not even notice.

For example, the way a person communicates with others, how people avoid confrontation when faced with problems or how nonverbal cues provide contextual meanings rather than textual. All the postgraduate students who contributed to my blog had illuminating stories to share about what it is like being an expatriate, and how to survive and thrive throughout the expatriation process. They are thus well equipped with a cadre of cultural competencies. Their divergent cultural values, high-context and low-context attitudes, and lively debates about personality vs. culture all helped me to advance my own thinking about how to express my ideas about culture, and to strengthen my understanding of the concept itself.

Reflecting on and analyzing the blog responses have made me even more convinced that culture has a great power to explain behaviour (though it may not be the only explanation). My students challenged my thinking whenever they were presented with a case to explain or asked to support their ideas about the topic of the week. My experiences on this blog as virtual class discussions have transformed many cultural encounters into realities that I had not imagined because of my own worldviews and cross-cultural experiences. The experience has helped all of us to apply the theory that we have learned.

The complexities of human nature may make some of the theoretical dimensions we discussed (see Chapter 2) seem impracticable, but the underlying assumptions prescribed by the theoretical lens are tools to solve the cultural dilemmas faced by SIEs. In essence, the knowledge-sharing activities that transpired on the blog result in in-depth discussions on managing across culture. The blog indeed offers an interesting virtual landscape to uncover and discover the many nuances and complexities of human beings that are associated with their cultural roots.

CULTURAL LESSON 10.2: SELF-INITIATED EXPATRIATES AS GLOBAL TALENTS: WHERE DO WE GO FROM HERE?

As expatriates shift from being an organization-initiated to a self-initiated phenomenon, many MNCs no longer limit their recruitment efforts to home-country nationals, but cast a global net to attract and recruit new talent. For the potential expatriate, the decision of whether they will be willing to relocate will depend on a number of factors, including the job environment and organizational culture, the reward package (financial and nonfinancial), the length of stay, the difficulties of the relocation process, and spousal and family support. For SIEs, there is also the question of whether there is any predeparture cross-cultural training available.

Crossing cultural boundaries into a foreign work environment is an exciting journey, but the adjustment process can be challenging. When an individual leaves their own culture and moves into another, they naturally bring along the "cultural baggage" of their historical background and personality. The situation is complicated further when language differences, lack of knowledge about the culture of the host country, or emotional reactions to new cultural sensitivities affect everyday life.

People who live in a foreign country for an extended period of time inevitably experience cultural stress; indeed, feelings of being overwhelmed or frustrated are a normal part of the cultural learning process. On top of this, many also experience homesickness for family and friends. Finally, when they return home, many expatriates find that their international assignment has disrupted their career (Bolino and Feldman, 2000; Caraher et al. 2007).

It is common for expatriates to experience culture shock when working abroad, but this can be overcome by adjusting to the new cultural environment. However, one of the primary reasons for the high failure rate among expatriates is the difficulty they find in making this adjustment (Garonzik et al. 2000; Takeuchi et al. 2007). Making a cultural adjustment is not easy; it takes time to change one's way of life and meet new friends. Martinen (2011) argued that cross-cultural adjustment can be measured in terms of emotional resilience, flexibility/openness and personal autonomy, which he identified as the characteristics required for effective cross-cultural interaction.

Martinen's model proposed three relatively independent dimensions of cross-cultural adjustment, namely work adjustment, interaction adjustment and general adjustment. Cross-cultural adjustment requires effort from both the expatriate and their spouse. Numerous studies have emphasized the importance of training individuals about the general and specific culture they will be joining, so that they acquire the right knowledge beforehand (Mendenhall and Stahl, 2000; Zakaria, 2000; Molinsky, 2007), though Wurtz (2014) noted that predeparture cross-cultural training has less of an impact on performance than in-country cross-cultural training. It appears that expatriates are more likely to be able to perform effectively if they are given adequate and relevant training upon arrival in the organization. Although predeparture training has previously been the norm for organization-assigned expatriates, it is less useful in aiding cross-cultural adjustment for SIEs.

The adjustment process is experienced differently by each expatriate. Over several stages of adaptation, SIEs will develop more realistic feelings toward and understanding of the new culture, and come to recognize both the similarities and the differences between the home and host cultures. The cultural adaptation process requires confidence, maturity, flexibility and tolerance on the part of the expatriate, but it will also be facilitated by having a good emotional support network. The ability to communicate in the local language and to stay in contact with family in the home country while also establishing a new network in the host country are key factors that promote swift cultural adjustments among SIEs. There are a few key areas where cross-cultural management researchers and international human resource management researchers might usefully concentrate their efforts:

- Financial motivations aside, what intrinsic factors drive SIEs to make the sacrifice to embark on a new career in a new work environment?

- What types of in-house and systematic cross-cultural training are provided by organizations when they recruit SIEs to ensure effective adjustment?
- What other cross-cultural competencies could be built into the career-development program of SIEs?
- In what ways does reverse adaptation for SIEs facilitate cross-cultural adjustment process?

CULTURAL LESSON 10.3: THE 3Cs OF THE SELF-INITIATED EXPATRIATE: CULTURE, CHANGE, COMPETENCIES

It is challenging to study culture, the concept of which has been defined by scholars in more than 160 ways. Oftentimes, culture produces intangible meanings that are abstract and difficult to comprehend or analyze, but examining its impact on behaviour can give us an insight into how a person thinks and feels. In this book, my key method for obtaining insights into expatriates' behaviours is the reflective practices approach. This relies on expatriates reflecting on a number of key questions; SIEs, for example, might contemplate the value of and need for change with reflective questions such as:

- Why do I need to change? Is change a necessity? Is the change permanent or temporary?
- To what extent is change necessary to my cross-cultural adjustment?
- What are the key aspects that I need to change? Which of these aspects do I need to prioritize?
- How critical are these aspects in ensuring successful cross-cultural adjustment?
- How long will the changes have to last for me to adapt to the new culture? How long will it take me to become culturally intelligent?
- In what ways could organizations change their structure and culture to facilitate SIE cross-cultural adjustment?

Change takes place at the individual, organizational and cultural levels. SIEs also need to change to develop cognitive, affective and behavioural competencies. My main assertion in this book is that culture impacts cross-cultural adjustment. Evidently, SIEs have to be prepared to change their mindset, have resilient emotions, and take appropriate actions since they need to fit into a new culture. As an end result, SIEs need to recognize that changes need to be endured, as cultural complexities persist! When the world is finally viewed as flat, cultural convergence may become a reality, but your own culture will remain important to you as well as for those who are working with you. As illustrated in the above blog vignette, SIEs who are equipped with cultural intelligence see that culture counts, and the 3Cs – culture, change and competencies – are considered the success criteria for the future generation of SIEs crossing different geographical boundaries as globally mobile talents.

After almost two decades of teaching about and researching culture and its impact on organizational behaviours, I am still constantly asking, "In what ways does culture play a role in our lives?" It is my firm belief that actively and positively engaging with other cultures can change our hearts; if that is the case, then our thoughts and actions will be integrated naturally, and we will learn to synchronize and harmonize the tempo and rhythm of our emotions and behaviours to fit the situation we are in, wherever and with whomever that may be. Hence, once we reach the mastery stage of acculturation, we can truly announce, "I am culturally intelligent!"

CULTURAL REFLECTION 10.1: THERE IS A GAP BETWEEN YOU AND ME!

Power distance is a cultural concept that explains the differing degree of inequality acceptance among people in an organization. This cultural dimension outlines the power order that exists between superiors and subordinates. This power is usually illustrated through the organizational structure, whether this is hierarchical or flat. In many contemporary organizational structures, the form is organic, and there is an emphasis on empowerment, decentralization and the minimization of bureaucracy.

Hofstede associated hierarchical structures with high power distance and flattened structures with low power distance. It is interesting to note that in reality, organizational structure explains less about a society's cultural values than about the way people observe or accept and interpret authority and power in the workplace. Organizational structures may change to suit the era of globalization, but culture tends to be more persistent in nature. For example, in my institution, people still maintain the hierarchical structure, and there is a high level of power distance between top management and the layers of management below. Other local companies have introduced the flattened structure, but there is still a culture of "gaps" between bosses and other staff.

- What do you think the concept of power means? How is power distributed in the workplace? Is there high or low power distance?
- How would you define your organizational structure? Can you provide examples?
- How hierarchical is the culture in your organization? Do you accept the boss as superior and that important decisions should be referred to them? If not, can you explain how it differs in your culture?
- Who normally makes decisions at work? How are these decisions made (what's the process)?
- How are you and your colleagues empowered within the organization?
- Who creates the organizational culture? The CEO alone or collectively with others in the organization?
    - Is it based on bureaucratic processes or processes that are co-constructed by members of the organization?
- In what ways does the organizational culture influence the way power is perceived and implemented by members of the organization?

CULTURAL REFLECTION 10.2: BETWEEN WORK AND PLAY?

Why is it that some people can clearly distinguish between work and personal, while some blur or don't see the lines between task and relationship? According to Trompenaars and Hampden-Turner (1997), a cultural dimension is called specific vs. diffuse, wherein a culture can be explained based on how people draw the boundary between work and personal life. This explains how relationships are viewed in the workplace. In Thailand, China and other Asian countries, people do not normally make a clear distinction between the role of friend and that of co-worker. The more established the personal relationship between a boss and his subordinates, the more highly motivated the subordinates will be to go all out to get the job done on time.

It also means that the practices for motivating subordinates, such as having a drink before or afterwards, or treating them while they are on the job, are already established. This is a common approach. I remember one time, we were requested by our director to do some overtime after normal working hours. As compensation, we were treated to a hefty lunch. That in itself seemed to boost my subordinate, who felt appreciated. The result was "enhanced spirit." In contrast, a culture that believes that work is work and play is play, and that one should not mix the two, will expect you to do the job, as long as it is within your capability and means, but it will not expect favours. In such a society, it is acceptable to say no.

- What does work mean to you? How do you define the job that you have to undertake?
- Do you see your relationships at work as friendships? Or do you see relationships as part of the task to be contributed together with your co-workers?
- Do you see a clear boundary between yourself and your superior? Or is this boundary blurred? Why is that so?
- The phrase "work is work and play is play" connotes a different level of trust (low or high). How do you interpret this phrase in the context of your culture?
- How do you see your work relationships as facilitating the work that you have to do?
- Are you relationship oriented at work or task oriented? How does this motivate you at work?
- How does this cultural value facilitate or hinder the level of trust between you and your colleagues?

10.1 @CULTURAL PONDERS

Culture: *I Learn, I Know, and It Does Makes Sense!*

Sarah Al Hashim
Autumn 2010

I believe that "different cultural values bring different perspectives to different people!" I know that in many respects, cultural values are not the only sources of success for expatriates. Personality can have a strong impact on qualities like resilience, persistence and perseverance when one faces the unknowns. I come from a collectivistic and high uncertainty avoidance culture; therefore, I am expected to act in this way. Truthfully speaking, my previous actions taken or decisions made, I have to really make sure that it was the safest decision I would take and try my best. If there is no need for that change, I wouldn't even bother to change it. Yet, through life experiences, I had to learn which ones that impact a change. Hence, I believe if a change is for the better and in the long-term will be a better decision I will make it even though it will be difficult and oppose the value culture I come from, because as a human being I do believe that change in different forms will be objected to at the beginning, but when the benefits become more clear, we tend to accept and adapt. In this regard, having the experience to go and live in another country and culture, I still did not have the chance of having this experience, as I had lived in UAE all my life, where I really feel that it is my home; even when I go to Jordan, which is my home country, I really don't feel that I belong there, maybe because all my family and most of my relatives are here in UAE, and usually I did get that chance to go there more frequently, but even though I always push myself to accept changes whatever they are, I feel it would be one of the biggest and hardest decisions in life.

References

Andresen, M., Bergdolt, F., Margenfeld, J., and Dickmann, M. 2014. Addressing international mobility confusion – developing definitions and differentiations for self-initiated and assigned expatriates as well as migrants. *The International Journal of Human Resource Management*, 25(16), 2295–2318.

Bolino, M.C. and Feldman, D.C. 2000. The antecedents and consequences of underemployment among expatriates, *Journal of Organizational Behavior*, 21(8), 889–911.

Carraher, S.M., Sullivan, S.E., and Crocitto, M.M. 2007, Mentoring across global boundaries: An empirical examination of home and host-country mentors on expatriate career outcomes. *Journal of International Business Studies*, 39(8), 1310–1326.

Chen, G.M. and Starosta, W.J. 1996. Intercultural communication competence: A synthesis. *Communication Yearbook*, 19, 353–383.

Deresky, H. 2008. *International Management: Managing Across Borders and Cultures*. Plattsburgh, NY: Pearson.

Earley, P.C., Ang, S., and Tan, J.-S. 2006. *CQ: Developing Cultural Intelligence at Work*. Palo Alto, CA: Stanford University Press.

Feldman, M. C. 2000. The antecedents and consequences of underemployment among expatriates. *Journal of Organizational Behavior*, 21(8), 889–911.

Garonzik, R., Brockner, J., and Siegel, P.A. 2000. Identifying international assignees at risk for premature departure: The interactive effect of outcome favorability and procedural fairness. *Journal of Applied Psychology*, 85(1), 13–20.

Gibbs, G. 1988. *Learning by Doing: A Guide to Teaching and Learning Methods*. Further Education Unit. Oxford: Oxford Polytechnic.

Goleman, D. 1996. Emotional intelligence. Why it can matter more than IQ. *Learning*, 24(6), 49–50.

Hall, E.T. 1959. *The Silent Language*, Garden City, NY: Doubleday.

Hall, E.T. 1976. *Beyond Culture*. New York: Anchor Books.

Hall, E.T. and Hall, M.R. 1990. *Understanding Cultural Differences – Germans, French and Americans*. Boston, MA: Intercultural Press.

Hofstede, G. 1984. *Culture's Consequences: International Differences in Work-Related Values*. Newbury Park, CA: Sage Publication Inc.

Hofstede, G. 1991. *Cultures and Organizations: Software of the Mind*. London: McGraw-Hill.

Hofstede, G. 2011. Dimensionalizing cultures: The Hofstede model in context. *Online Readings in Psychology and Culture*, 2(1). doi:10.9707/2307-0919.1014

Hooker, J. 2003. *Working Across Cultures*, Stanford, CA: Stanford Press Publisher.

Kenichi, O. 1990. *The Borderless World: Power and Strategy in the Global Marketplace*. New York: Harper Collins.

Kolb, D.A. 1984. *Experiential Learning: Experience as the Source of Learning and Development*. Englewood Cliffs, NJ: Prentice-Hall.

Kroeber, A.L. and Kluckhohn, C. 1952. *Culture: A Critical Review of Concepts and Definitions*. Cambridge, MA: Peabody Museum.

Lysgaard, S. 1955. Adjustment in a foreign society: Norwegian Fulbright grantees visiting the United States. *International Social Science Bulletin*, 7, 45–51.

Martinen, R. 2011. Predicting changes in cultural sensitivity among students of Spanish during short-term study abroad. *Hispania*, 1(March), 121–141.

Maslow, A. H. 1943. A theory of human motivation. *Psychological Review*, 50, 370–396.

Mendenhall, M. and Stahl, M.E. 2000. Expatriate training and development: Where do we go from here? *Human Resource Management*, 39(2–3), 251–265.

Minkov, M. and Hofstede, G. 2011. The evolution of Hofstede doctrine. *Cross-cultural Management: An International Journal*, 18(1), 10–20.

Molinsky, A. 2007. Cross-cultural code-switching: The psychological challenges of adapting behavior in foreign cultural interactions. *Academy of Management Review*, 32(2), 622–640.

Ohmae, K. 1990. *The Borderless World: Power and Strategy in the Interlinked Economy*. New York: Harper Business.

Ohmae, K. 2005. *The Next Global Stage: Challenges and Opportunities in Our Borderless World*. Cranbury, NJ: Pearson Education.

Osland, J.S. and Bird, A. 2000. Beyond sophisticated stereotyping: Cross-cultural sensemaking in context. *Academy of Management Executive*, 14, 1–12.

Osland, J.S. and Bird, A. 2003. Beyond sophisticated stereotyping: Cultural sensemaking in context. In: Thomas, D.C. (Ed.), *Readings and Cases in International Management: A Cross-Cultural Perspective*. Thousand Oaks, CA: Sage, p. 58.

Richardson, J. 2004. Self-directed expatriation: Family matters. *Personnel Review*, 35(4), 469–486.

Riki Takeuchi, D.P. 2007. Nonlinear influences of stressors on general adjustment: the case of Japanese expatriates and their spouses. *Journal of International Business Studies*, 38(6), 928–943.

Schein, E. 1984. Coming to a new awareness of organizational culture. *Sloan Management Review*, 25(2), 3–16.

Schwartz, S.H. 1992. *Universals in the Content and Structure of Values: Theoretical Advances and Empirical Tests in 20 Countries*. San Diego, CA: Academic Press.

Shawn, M. and Carraher, S.E. 2008. Mentoring across global boundaries: an empirical examination of home- and host-country mentors on expatriate career outcomes. *Journal of International Business Studies*, 39(8), 1310–1326.

Stahl, M.E. 2000. Expatriate training and development: Where do we go from here? *Human Resource Management*, 39(2–3), 251–265.

Takeuchi, R., Lepak, D.P., Marinova, S.V., and Yun, S. 2007. Nonlinear influences of stressors on general adjustment: The case of Japanese expatriates and their spouses. *Journal of International Business Studies*, 38(6), 928–943.

Ting-Toomey, S. 1999. *Communicating across Cultures*. New York: Guilford Press.

Trompenaars, F. and Hampden-Turner, C. 1997. *Riding the Waves of Culture: Understanding Cultural Diversity in Business*. London: Nicholas Brealey.

Trompenaars, F., and Hampden-Turner, C. 1997. *Riding the Waves of Culture*. London: McGraw-Hill.

Unegbu, V.E. and Onuoha, U.D. 2013. Globalization lessons from review of Ohmae's *The Next Global Stage: Challenges and Opportunities in Our Borderless World*. *Journal of Law, Policy and Globalization*, 11, 36–42.

Wurtz, O. 2014. An empirical investigation of the effectiveness of pre-departure and in-country cross-cultural training. *The International Journal of Human Resource Management*, 25(14), 2088–2101.

Zakaria, N. 2000. The effects of cross-cultural training on the acculturation process of the global workforce. *International Journal of Manpower,* 21(6), 492–510.

Zakaria, N., Stanton, J. and Sarkar-Barney, S.T.M. 2003. Designing and implementing culturally-sensitive IT applications: The interaction of culture values and privacy issues in the Middle East. *Information, Technology & People,* 16(1), pp. 49–75.

Zakaria, N. 2008. What does it take? New praxes of cross-cultural competency for global virtual teams as innovative work structure. In: S. Kundu and S. Munjal. (Eds.), *Human Capital and Innovation: Palgrave Studies in Global Human Capital Management.* London: Palgrave Macmillan, pp. 131–160.

Zakaria, N. 2017. *Culture Matters? Decision Making in Global Virtual Teams: Managing the Challenges and Synergies during Globally Distributed Collaboration.* Boca Raton, FL: CRC Press.

Index

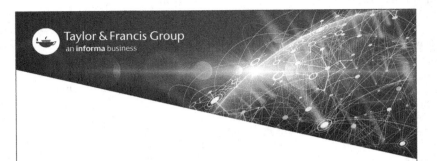

Printed in the United States
by Baker & Taylor Publisher Services